BEYOND SURVIVAL TO THRIVING

EMPOWERING STORIES & ADVICE FROM WOMEN BALANCING FAITH, CAREER S, BUSINESS AND RELATIONSHIPS

TABLE OF CONTENTS

SECTION ONE

THRIVING IN SINGLENESS

WHEN LOVE BECOMES A BUSINESS

SONDRIA GIORDANI

Being a single woman, is a freedom I wouldn't trade for the world. Would it be nice to marry the right spouse? Yes. But I'd rather wait for the right one. I'm 45 and have no regrets. For now, my business is my form of love. Yes, I had goals. I wanted to start a rental business alongside being a Pediatric Nurse, and I was also interested in investing in stocks. But I guess God had different plans for me when I gave my life to Him in 2013.

In 2012, my mom suffered a mild heart attack and needed a coronary artery bypass. It was one of my greatest pains. She survived the surgery, but between 2012 and 2015, I took a lot of time off work to care for her during her illness. By March 2015, I received a letter calling for my resignation. I was told beforehand that it was either my job or my mother. For me, it wasn't a choice—it was a deliverance. I just didn't realize it at the time. I remember sitting on the sofa, reading that letter, feeling confused. I stood up and thought, "Why is this happening to me?" I didn't consider myself a bad person who deserved all these hardships. Then, I heard a voice in my right ear saying, "Read the book of Job." I had never read the book of Job because I was focused on the New Testament. But I opened the Bible and read Job. At the time, I was unemployed with only $8,000 in savings.

I called HR at the hospital where I worked, and they allowed me to take my retirement savings, which was just $25,000. Between budgeting what I had and what my mom contributed, we were able to maintain both her house and mine. It was a tight budget, and I thank God I've always been a frugal person. I like to live below my means. My mortgage was only $985, with $200 for HOA fees, plus utilities and car insurance. Excluding gas and groceries, my monthly budget was $1,731. I'm not going to lie—there were moments when I worried about not making it or running out of money. But God constantly reminded me of Matthew 6, and it became my anthem.

Caring for my mom became my full-time job. She was constantly in and out of hospitals and clinics. It was rough because I wanted my life back, and so did she. But during this time, I learned to be sacrificial, patient, and spiritually strong. I grew in my relationship with God, debated His word, and denied myself things I didn't need. I also became sharper with my finances through financial classes. Two weeks before my mom passed, the Lord gave me Psalm 23. She died in July 2017, and I am thankful to God that He gave me peace and fulfillment. I have no regrets. The greatest gift I received was time.

After I buried my mom, I was ready to start my life again. I applied for clinic jobs and began looking into real estate investments for my rental business. I also invested the money my mom left me in stocks and a Roth IRA. I got an interview call for a clinic job at a university in Boca, but the Lord interrupted me. In a dream, He expressed concern about my brother, Thomas. It was a struggle—choosing between getting my life back or dealing with someone's salvation. I made the choice not to go to the interview and to hold off on the real estate investment. The Lord doesn't always give you all the details. He may show you the end, but you rarely know the steps to get there.

I had a different idea about giving Thomas—my baby brother— the salvation story, imagining it would happen in the hospital. But God had other plans. Thomas was 33, a petty drug dealer, a woman-beater, a thief, someone who smoked weed all night and slept all day. Thankfully, he was a terrible shot, so murder never made it onto his résumé. Thomas had both good and bad in him. I gave him resources to help him become more responsible and accountable, to manage finances, and to maintain a household. I wanted him to grow into adulthood because my mom had him like a baby.

Crippled and handicapped—I wanted him to appreciate the things my mom did for us. He did well for two years until he decided to have a shootout at a gas station, which was kept a secret from me. By then, I was running out of money, four years into this. I had started with $160,000 after paying for my mom's funeral, taxes, tithes, and offerings. By April 2020, I believe I was down to $600. I prayed hard, sitting on my sofa, hoping someone would call with good news. I sure do like to eat.

One day, I was watching Maldonado on TV, where people were testifying about God's goodness. I said to myself, "I'm joining this team." So, I got online and applied for COVID relief. Then one morning, the bank sent someone to the house. He caught me while I was taking out the garbage. I wasn't happy at all, but it actually worked in my favor. I mustered the strength to call the bank, and they were so helpful during COVID. They gave me a forbearance. This all happened around September and October of 2020. Everything got paid—mortgage, electricity, water, HOA fees. Food was stocked in the refrigerator and pantry, enough to last a year.

Then, on February 7th, 2021, I got the call from my cousin that Thomas had passed. I was shocked because I thought I would meet him at the hospital. It turned out God had a different strategy. I like to call it a homeless ministry because it felt like we were doing the same run. But Thomas had the same privileges as I did. He repented the night he passed. The Lord told me in a dream, "He won." In a previous dream, He had also told me Thomas would be with my mom.

I wish I were finished. So far, it's been six years of unemployment. I buried Thomas on April 1st, 2021. Then the Lord interrupted me again with another dream—this time about my dad and his son, and a little girl wishing for something. I need God to put me on His payroll because this is not an easy job, and the compensation isn't matching. So, I spent another two years sitting on my sofa, praying and ministering to my dad and his ex-wife about their son—dealing with demons and witchcraft and backing it up with the Bible. I told the Lord, "No more Matthew 6," but He gave me Psalm 23 again. I felt like I was living the story of the two fish and five loaves ministry. I received many miracles.

I was in a bad car accident involving a drunk driver, and even the attorney couldn't comprehend how it happened based on the video footage. She said the accident didn't make sense. The end of 2022 was difficult but manageable. I did have to sell my house due to the fight over my mom's house and money, but the Lord kept me together and gave me peace. After selling my house, I told the Lord, "I want luxury and nothing less."

Now, I'm working at a great clinic, investing in stocks, writing Christian children's books, and providing encouragement to young girls and women through my Instagram, little_tiaras_in_the_making—a community for radical kingdom women and girls. Hopefully, sometime next year, I'll also start my rental business.

Advice I would give to women and men:

- **Prioritize what's truly important.** Do you value life or material things?

- **Sharpen your discernment skills.** You never want to fund Satan's kingdom while thinking it's God's.

- **Learn to evaluate your needs versus wants.** Don't purchase things unless they are necessary or can be used regularly.

- **Master your emotions and be honest with God.** He can help balance you with His truth and understanding. I like to tell the Lord I'd rather be honest than end up like Cain.

- **Learn to be patient and still.** It's hard if you like to stay busy, but patience reveals what is real and what is not. Deception doesn't last long, but truth does.

- **Be creative—it saves money.** You'd be surprised how God can give you solutions.

A JOURNEY TO ENTREPRENEURSHIP

SEYA WILSON

The future favors the brave"—these words echo a timeless truth, emphasizing the limitless possibilities that await those bold enough to take decisive steps. For me, this means that embracing bravery not only propels us toward unforeseen opportunities but also shapes the very fabric of our destiny. In bravery, we take risks that can forever alter the course of our lives.

In December 2019, I made a bold decision that would set the course for my future: I wanted to give myself the opportunity to live outside of Jamaica and further my education. However, I was fully aware that funding a Master's degree in the United States or Canada was beyond my financial reach without external assistance at that time in my life. The Commonwealth Scholarship Commission of the UK seemed like an ideal solution, so I set out to research this opportunity. This involved applying to and gaining acceptance at a university in a country where the scholarship would cover tuition fees. I chose to apply to a university in South Africa, a country whose history and culture I had always admired. I vividly remember the excitement and passion surrounding Nelson Mandela's visit to Jamaica in 1991, an event that profoundly shaped my perception of South Africa. The lead-up to the end of Apartheid and Nelson Mandela's release after 27 years in prison attracted global attention, and South Africa's first democratic election in 1994 ignited excitement in Jamaica, as our shared struggle for justice was realized.

Little did I know that years later, I would have a date with destiny—a journey that would radically reshape my perspective on life and goal-setting. Although I didn't secure the scholarship, I was accepted into the University of Johannesburg in South Africa, with admission starting in February 2020. To say I was confused and uncertain would be an understatement, but, as with every challenging decision I've faced, I confronted this one head-on. At the same time, I was at a crossroads in my career, seeking new opportunities for growth, skill acquisition, and passion alignment. I felt the need for change, but I wondered, how could I facilitate a move to another hemisphere while also expanding my earning potential? My financial stability would play a major role in my ability to relocate and successfully complete my studies. As I journaled through this process, I recall the inner conflict I felt—almost as if I had to give myself an ultimatum to choose one path or the other.

This is where the first lesson in the process emerged. Just as the internal conflict heightened, I reminded myself of the invaluable role of one's network. I reached out to Dr. Joan Wright Good, a long-time family friend, to share my thoughts and seek her guidance.

She guided me through a process that only a seasoned business coach or someone deeply familiar with this journey could offer. I remember how that session brought clarity to my thoughts, helping me understand my passions, strengths, and the need to align them with potential opportunities in the service industry. This realization was both enlightening and critical for me as a prospective business owner at the time. I left the conversation convinced that, along with our network, our skills and passions are among our greatest assets. It's often said, "Your network is your net worth," and learning how to leverage your talents can unlock numerous opportunities.

I was confident in my strengths, but monetizing them was a different story. This led me to another important lesson: anything can be monetized. If you possess a skill or a passion, there is usually a market for it. The key is finding the right way to package and present it.

In the months following my decision, I embarked on a thorough self-assessment to identify my core strengths and passions. This process was both enlightening and affirming. I began to realize that my unique abilities and experiences weren't just valuable—they were profitable.

Whether through freelance work, consulting, or launching a new small business, my mind opened to the endless possibilities.

As I prepared for my journey to South Africa, I also began exploring various entrepreneurial avenues. This dual focus—continuing my education while seeking to establish a business—was challenging but invigorating. It was a time of immense personal growth, where I learned the importance of resilience, adaptability, and, above all, faith. My Christian beliefs were a constant source of strength and guidance, reminding me that I wasn't alone in this journey, even when things didn't unfold as I had ideally planned.

It was when a friend introduced me to a famous Karl Marx quote that I truly understood the monumental skill set required for advancement in any area of life. The quote reads: "Men can be distinguished from animals by consciousness, by religion, or anything else you like. They themselves begin to distinguish themselves from animals as soon as they begin to produce their means of subsistence, a step which is conditioned by their physical organization."

This means that what sets humans apart is their ability to consciously plan and produce what they need for survival, driven by their inherent capabilities and creativity. Identifying what one wants to achieve is only the beginning; planning the journey is the second step. But the true test of a person lies in their ability to organize themselves and make steady progress toward their goal. It's the ability to rise each day and take small steps toward the vision of the life we hope to create—nothing more, nothing less.

With this in mind, while still in Jamaica, I founded Virtual Global Outsourcers Incorporated in January 2020. This was my sole New Year's resolution, and I set out to manifest a year full of opportunities. With my first client on board, I embarked on my journey as a Virtual Assistant, leveraging my strong administrative skills to serve clients globally. I focused specifically on small business clients, referred to me through my network. One of the greatest business insights I gained during this process was the understanding that "your good name will carry you farther than any other description, and keeping it intact will take you far."

This all unfolded as I was preparing to leave for my studies two months later. By then, my internal conflicts were resolved—I was determined to earn and pursue higher education simultaneously, without a doubt, or so I thought.

The Balance of Faith and Entrepreneurship

"Or so I thought." This sentiment resonates deeply as I reflect on the intertwined journey of faith and entrepreneurship. Being a Christian demands unwavering submission to faith. As stated in Hebrews 11:1, "faith is the substance of things hoped for, the evidence of things not seen." If I could relive those moments, I'd plaster sticky notes with this verse all over my space as constant reminders. My early entrepreneurial days were far from embodying Hebrews 11:1. Instead, uncertainty dominated.

Launching a new business inherently involves navigating uncharted waters, with challenges that no amount of preparation can fully address. Despite these uncertainties, I pressed on, driven by the realization that much of the learning happens on the job. Through trial and error, I uncovered a key truth: nothing is beyond reach if you commit to learning. "Never say you don't know" became my personal mantra, and every unknown became an opportunity to gain knowledge. And learn, I did.

By March 2020, just as my business was gaining momentum, the world was hit with an unprecedented crisis—the coronavirus pandemic. The term "novel" carried profound weight; it was both unfamiliar and terrifying. My faith was put to the test.

Just days before my scheduled move to South Africa, with my fledgling business in tow, the world came to a sudden halt. My flight was canceled, and uncertainty loomed large. In that moment, I grappled with questions of grace and resilience. How would I find the strength to move forward? Yet, through divine providence, the path began to clear. Unbeknownst to me, the pandemic's challenges birthed new virtual business opportunities. I began assisting other businesses in their pivots, offering services to help them navigate the abrupt transition to virtual operations.

This newfound avenue of virtual consultancy revealed an unexpected gift—the ability to support others during an exceptionally turbulent time. Our shared challenges fostered mutual success, sparking a powerful and positive synergy.

Even as my business grew, the demands of entrepreneurship were closely intertwined with my academic pursuits. Attending online classes brought its own set of challenges, especially with the 7-hour time difference between South Africa and Jamaica. Weekday mornings required early starts as I juggled my educational commitments alongside the evolving demands of my business.

Maintaining a balance between faith and entrepreneurship required constant reinforcement. In the midst of chaos, faith became my anchor. Hebrews 11:1 served as a guiding principle, reminding me to hope and believe in the unseen. My journey highlighted the importance of staying steadfast in faith, particularly when navigating the uncertainties of entrepreneurship during a global pandemic. The delicate yet essential balance between faith and business involved trusting divine timing, embracing uncertainties, and evolving through challenges.

Looking back, the path was anything but straightforward. Yet every detour and obstacle strengthened my faith and sharpened my entrepreneurial spirit. This journey proved that faith and entrepreneurship are not mutually exclusive; instead, they complement each other in profound and transformative ways. However, there were still unexpected turns throughout the ensuing years.

The Challenges of a Single Professional Woman and Business Owner

As the pandemic stretched on, the phrase "new normal" became ubiquitous. Wave after wave of COVID-19, along with mounting casualties, forced a stark understanding of our mortality.

Trapped in place by perpetual lockdowns, restlessness grew—what's next? Amid the mix of skepticism, conspiracy theories, and claims of population control or divine intervention, one fact remained: COVID-19 impacted lives and livelihoods across all boundaries.

I knew that once this crisis ended—and end it must—I would need to start afresh. It wasn't that my business was failing; rather, I had acquired new skills by working with clients, which broadened my service offerings. I also realized that if I wanted my company to grow, I could no longer operate as a one-woman band; I needed to bring on a few subcontractors.

As the daily number of pandemic casualties began to decline, borders reopened, and the focus shifted to resuming normal life. Forecasts warned that COVID-19 would have lasting effects, including a surge in mental health conditions like PTSD. Despite this, many people rushed to regain a sense of normalcy. Yet, lingering thoughts persisted. I constantly asked myself, "What if?" Having made it through the pandemic relatively unscathed, I found myself grappling with new anxieties. Chief among these was a heightened sense of vulnerability as an unmarried young woman with a child.

This realization extended into my entrepreneurial ventures. I understood that being single left me without safety nets. What if things hadn't worked out? I had neither a backup plan nor a built-in support system. This mindset profoundly influenced my business decisions and personal life.

One significant challenge was balancing my professional responsibilities with my personal life. Unlike my married counterparts, I lacked a partner for emotional and financial support. As a result, every business decision required meticulous planning to ensure stability for both me and my child. The absence of a safety net meant the stakes were higher; any misstep could have serious consequences.

Another obstacle was the bias and skepticism I encountered as a single female entrepreneur. Despite the growing number of women in business, stereotypes persisted. I often faced questions about whether I could effectively manage both motherhood and a growing enterprise. This skepticism forced me to constantly prove my competence—not just to clients, but also to potential business partners.

Networking, an essential aspect of business growth, presented its own challenges. Many networking events remained male-dominated, making it difficult to find relatable mentors or peers. Building a professional support system required extra effort and perseverance. Without guided mentorship, I often had to learn lessons the hard way.

At the time, I believed that marriage would provide a safety net—after all, two is better than one. I also realized I was frequently using my friends as personal sounding boards, sharing the weight of my business development roles. I saw this as a consequence of being unmarried, thinking that support and encouragement would be more effectively channeled through a partner.

While these thoughts occasionally crossed my mind, my vision remained steadfast. They were reflections, not constant worries, but they surfaced whenever challenges arose.

Upon accepting the invitation to contribute to this anthology, I reflected on how the journey had unfolded exactly as it was meant to, including my singleness. I rejoiced in how God has guided me, even when the narrative didn't match my expectations. As Hebrews 13:20-21 reminds us, "God will equip you with everything good for doing His will, and may He work in us what is pleasing to Him, through Jesus Christ, to whom be glory forever and ever."

As long as you earn a living honestly, with integrity, and trust in God, this is pleasing to Him, and He will equip us along the way. For those of us who are presently unmarried, despite the challenges, we are supported in other ways. It's perfectly fine to share with trusted friends, hire a coach, consult with experts, and explore ways to strengthen financial security. We must utilize the resources God has provided for us.

During this time, I realized that in the next phase of my business, transitioning from a sole proprietorship to a partnership might be a viable option.

Managing the Work-Life Balance

In 2022, I expanded my business and rebranded it as The Virtual Office Hub, marking a period of tremendous growth. One day, during a client call, I had an epiphany: I was no longer just assisting with administration. I had evolved into a marketing consultant, business development specialist, and project manager, offering digital transformation services to businesses. This realization excited me, especially because I was now able to afford subcontractors.

At this time, the world was still adjusting to the aftermath of COVID-19, with remote work becoming the norm. My new team allowed me to take a more hands-off approach to daily operations. My son was eight years old, and the flexibility in my schedule allowed me to be more present during school pickups and provide better supervision in the afternoons. However, I occasionally found myself drawn back into day-to-day tasks, creating an ebb and flow that persisted.

A seasoned business professional once told me, "If you cannot operate a business without being constantly present, then it's not a business; it's just you." Those words resonated deeply with me and motivated me to build a self-sustaining business.

Balancing client demands with personal responsibilities became a daily challenge. Clients expect deliverables regardless of what's happening in your personal life. To create more efficiency, I recalibrated our systems, updated standard operating procedures, and improved both business and client reporting structures. Over time, I was able to set clearer boundaries around work hours. After-hours and weekends were strictly designated as personal time, and I no longer felt guilty about not pouring every moment into the business I was so passionate about.

Furthering my studies in South Africa introduced its own challenges, particularly due to the ongoing load-shedding crisis caused by electricity shortages. This additional complexity made it crucial for me to establish stricter time management and set clearer boundaries. My commitment to maintaining a balance between my business and personal life only deepened.

The ability to delegate and trust my team became essential. I shifted from being constantly hands-on to focusing more on strategy and growth. This transition allowed me to dedicate quality time to my son and be more present in his life, especially during the afternoons after school pickups.

Maintaining work-life balance also meant recognizing when to step away. I began incorporating regular breaks into my day to avoid burnout. Setting boundaries around work hours was initially challenging, but it paid off significantly. Clients were informed of these limitations, and expectations were managed accordingly.

This new approach not only reduced stress but also reignited my enjoyment of work. I found that I was more productive and creative when there were clear distinctions between work and personal time.

Reflecting on the advice from the seasoned business practitioner, I came to understand the importance of building a self-sustaining business. It wasn't just about stepping away; it was about ensuring that operations continued seamlessly without my constant involvement. This was the true test of efficient systems and strong team management.

Mentorship & Giving Back

In 2022, I finally arrived in South Africa to continue my studies, which brought a whole new set of challenges. One of the major issues was load-shedding due to the electricity crisis, which significantly affected my day-to-day life. The time difference between South Africa and my home country presented another hurdle, complicating my scheduling and communication with clients.

As my academic responsibilities increased, I had to make the difficult decision to narrow my client base. This felt like a setback since I was just starting to see profits from my business, but it was a necessary step to ensure I could effectively manage all my commitments.

To stay on top of everything, I had to become more disciplined with my time. I dedicated specific periods to study, business, and personal life, adhering to a strict schedule to meet various deadlines. This phase taught me valuable lessons in balancing priorities, as I found a way to make it all work—because it simply had to, and there was no room for negotiation.

In 2023, I decided to close the chapter on my previous business model. It had outgrown its purpose, and it was time to rebrand

and move in a new direction. I shared this vision with my best friend, Rayharna Wright, and together we embarked on a new venture—creating a knowledge processing outsourcing company. This led to the birth of Sourcify, a group of companies operating in both Jamaica and the United States.

However, the journey toward establishing Sourcify began long before. As I was preparing to go to South Africa, I often contemplated how I could share my extensive knowledge with small business owners. Many of these entrepreneurs were limited by their financial circumstances and needed insights into business trends to help them grow. I felt a responsibility to share my experiences and knowledge with those who could benefit from them.

To address this need, I launched the Virtual Boss Academy and its accompanying Virtual Boss online webinar series. The goal was to provide affordable yet comprehensive business education to small business owners. The first season of the webinar series was a resounding success, with over 100 small business owners gaining valuable knowledge through various courses offered at a minimal fee.

Through the Virtual Boss Academy, I aimed to simplify core business concepts and offer actionable insights that entrepreneurs could immediately apply. Topics covered included financial management, digital marketing, customer service, and strategic planning. The feedback was overwhelmingly positive, with many participants reporting significant improvements in their business operations and growth after implementing what they had learned.

Moving forward, I am committed to continuing this form of giving back. Knowledge has been my greatest tool for business development, helping me offer more to my clients and stay ahead in a competitive market. By sharing what I've learned, I hope to empower other entrepreneurs to achieve their business goals and aspirations.

This mentorship and educational outreach are deeply fulfilling. They not only enable me to give back to the community but also allow me to stay connected with the grassroots realities of small business owners. This connection, in turn, enriches my own understanding and keeps me grounded in the practicalities of running a business.

As Sourcify grows and evolves, the principles of mentorship and knowledge-sharing remain at the core of its mission. It's not just about outsourcing services; it's about creating a robust ecosystem where businesses can thrive by leveraging shared knowledge and collective experiences.

This is how I thrive!

AUTISM
AN UNEXPECTED JOURNEY

SHANEKA NELSON

When my marriage ended, it reshaped the way I parented, sharpening my instincts and making me more vigilant than ever. As a mother, I had always been a natural protector and nurturer, but the divorce intensified these instincts. I wasn't just responsible for ensuring my child felt loved and cared for anymore; I had to be everything— provider, protector, nurturer—all on my own. There was no partner to share the weight, no one to bounce ideas off of or to step in when I needed a break. I became the backup plan, and this realization made me acutely aware of every decision I made. Failure wasn't an option.

Then came the storm of emotions when I learned that my child was on the spectrum. The guilt was overwhelming. I kept asking myself: was it something I did or didn't do? Anger followed swiftly: why my child? For days, I was paralyzed, weighed down by the enormity of it all. I prayed for understanding and clarity, seeking guidance from God on how to move forward.

Autism wasn't a topic we discussed in my world. Before my daughter's diagnosis, I had only heard the term "autistic" once. The doctor warned me that my child might never speak. But then, just a week after that diagnosis, something incredible happened. As I played Maranda Curtis's song "You Are My Strength," I heard my child singing along. The child who had been labeled nonverbal was singing! That moment was a beacon of hope and strength for me. It felt as though God was whispering, "Shaneka, I'm not done with you yet." From that day on, I threw myself into learning about autism and how best to support those on the spectrum.

As I delved deeper, I discovered I wasn't alone in facing these challenges. Many parents, especially single mothers like me, struggled with the same issues—chief among them, a lack of support. My family was there for me, but asking someone to babysit for an hour was a far cry from what I really needed. This was a different game altogether. My greatest fear was that my daughter would be misunderstood. People on the spectrum are often unfairly labeled as rude, lazy, or selfish, when in reality, they simply perceive the world differently. Their brains work in unique ways, and it's up to us to educate those around them. I found myself teaching friends, family, and even strangers how to interact with my daughter when she didn't respond as expected. Finding appropriate childcare, extracurricular activities, or playdates was another struggle. Not everyone has the patience or understanding needed to support someone on the spectrum, and that's where my real battle lay.

Despite the challenges, I'm both humbled and grateful for what I've accomplished. I've built a successful real estate business and become a homeowner—two legacies I'm proud to leave for my daughter. But beyond these material achievements, what fulfills me the most is knowing that I'm paving the way for her future. I wasn't raised in a family where we talked about stocks, life insurance, or real estate. Yet here I am, passing down that knowledge and setting up a foundation for my child. That is my greatest achievement—giving her the tools I never had.

If there's one lesson I've learned, it's this: never give up on yourself. Growing up on the small island of Kingston, Jamaica, I never imagined I'd find myself in rooms with multi-millionaires or sitting at tables where significant decisions are made. But I did—because I believed in myself and my purpose. I refused to let a failed relationship halt my growth. I didn't let the unknowns of autism stop me from learning. I didn't let the chatter of gossipers derail me. I kept my focus, competed only with myself, and persevered every single day.

To any parent, especially single parents of children with special needs, my advice is simple: advocate. Never give up. Don't let anyone define your child or place limits on their potential. Every day, I have my daughter recite affirmations, ensuring she says them with conviction. The world often pushes people to fit in or fall aside. It's my job to make sure my daughter never falls aside. Whether it's at school, church, therapy, hobbies, or even when we travel, I will always be there to guide and speak up for her when she cannot.

Finally, let's talk about self-care—something I didn't prioritize for far too long. As a single mom, finding time for myself seemed impossible, and eventually, it took a toll on me both mentally and physically. I'm a planner, and if I knew then what I know now, I would have scheduled at least one day a month for a full reset—a day with no work, no calls, no cooking, just rest. It's often overlooked, but self-care is essential. Even God rested.

As you journey through life, remember that it's okay to pause and take care of yourself. Doing so is not just an act of self-love; it's a gift to those who depend on you.

SECTION TWO

THRIVING IN **MARRIAGE**

YOU CAN THRIVE IN MARRIAGE

CHERYL RIVIERA

As I begin to share the intimate details of my marriage, July 2024 marks 34 years of being married to the same man. In Christendom, there's a common saying: "Only God can do it!" But I'd like to put it the way I feel it—"Only God can take your disorder and bring order." According to Merriam-Webster, survival means the ability to know what to do to stay alive.

Dear friend, this was my life for the first 26 years of our marriage. We knew how to survive but not how to thrive. Of course, no one enters marriage expecting to start in survival mode. When a man loves you, it brings such peace, making you feel safe and secure. That's how I feel now.

But I'm not sure I felt completely safe and secure before our wedding day. I thought maybe it was just wedding nerves. All I knew was that we were in love and committed to serving the

Lord. Yet, the first few years were so hard. We had our first daughter a year after we married, and our second daughter two years later.

We had no clue what we were doing. All we knew was that we loved each other. But I kept asking myself, why do I have to start every conversation with, How are we going to pay the bills? Do you realize the rent and the electric bill are due? We must pay our tithes. Yes, I said all this in one breath—no exaggeration.

We attended every church service, and I thought we should lead a Bible study. I even wanted my husband to do everything like Brother Watermelon did. Meanwhile, my role as a loving wife was slowly turning into that of a boss. I thought the way to keep our marriage alive was by keeping my husband in check. It breaks my heart to reflect on how I sounded back then.

I was cutting into my husband's ego and stripping him of his masculinity. When he couldn't come up with a plan, I'd use scripture and say things like, "You are the man; you're supposed to be the head of this house." Yet, I was the one making the decisions.

When all of my solutions failed, my anxiety would rise. My fear would turn into sharp words that cut deep, causing more pain. Looking back now, I realize it was fear driving me. Why couldn't I just keep my mouth shut? Where was my help? Where was the Holy Spirit? Looking back, I'm guessing I grieved Him too.

Despite the challenges, I remain humbled and grateful for all that we have accomplished together. Our daughters brought us so much joy, even as we struggled financially. They filled us with the love we needed when we felt like the weight of the world was on our shoulders. We were determined not to fail in our marriage. Weekends felt like a breath of fresh air, giving us brief moments to escape the pressures of bills and responsibilities. But the reality of not knowing how we would pay the next round of expenses always loomed over us, casting a shadow on even the brightest of days.

As the stress mounted, I could see my husband withdrawing more and more. He went along with whatever I said, but deep down, I knew he was frustrated—frustrated with not having enough money and with hearing too much of my nagging. We spent years struggling, faithfully serving our church and others, but keeping our hardships to ourselves. Pride wouldn't let me admit to our church family that we were struggling.

Still, I believe God honored our servant hearts because, somehow, a way was always made.

Then, years later, my husband's company, Mortola, had a massive layoff. He decided to pursue a degree in Information Technology, all while serving as our youngest daughter's full-time caregiver. Meanwhile, my professional career was advancing, and eventually, my husband earned his degree. Our finances finally took a turn for the better.

But even with more money, we hadn't changed our behavior—no goal setting, no weekly planning, no vision for our family. We were caught in the endless cycle of work, church, and school—wash, rinse, repeat. Life wasn't all gloom and doom. We had good times with our church friends and enjoyed family outings. But maintaining our household was a constant struggle—it had become our normal. It was like having a friend who was always around but never added any real value to your life.

As our income increased, I couldn't help but ask, "What is wrong, Lord?" We had more money, but we were still struggling. It took me years to understand the truth that if you don't assign your money a purpose, it will dictate its own direction. My spiritual father later taught me this important lesson. We spent three tough years digging ourselves out of the financial hole we had fallen into. But slowly, things started to look up. We moved out of the hood and into two beautiful properties. Around that time, I started attending a church that taught the resurrected Christ and God's plan for us to prosper.

I began to learn that we were worthy of all the promises of God—that we could subdue and have dominion. Let me tell you,

I experienced a paradigm shift. God blessed me with a spiritual father, Bishop Hugh Thomas, now living in eternity. He taught me many

things, but the most significant guidance he gave was to know who God is and to welcome the Holy Spirit into my life. I began to read the Bible more and more, and my life started to transform. I saw everything more clearly. We stayed with this church for 16 years. The enemy comes to kill, steal, and destroy, but God wants us to have life more abundantly.

I learned to go beyond merely surviving and start thriving. I chose to be a spirit-led being rather than a religious one. Before this, I hadn't been growing in the fruits of the Spirit or displaying the image of God. I didn't truly know the Holy Spirit. In my blindness, I had become like a Pharisee—religious-minded but spiritually stagnant. Our lack of planning had given the enemy plenty of room to operate, trapping us in both financial and spiritual bondage. Yet, through it all, I remained faithful to the word marriage.

In this new church, I did a lot of spiritual work, which helped reveal my own heart. Both my husband and I carried baggage, disappointments, and past traumas. We needed restoration— neither of us was equipped to handle all the responsibilities that come with marriage and raising children. In hindsight, I realize I was more in love with the idea of being in love than with the reality of it. But finally, clarity began to emerge.

Then, everything shifted. Shock and confusion hit me when I lost my dream job working with the United States Tennis Association. It felt like a punch in the chest. Now, my husband had to carry the load alone. We found ourselves struggling again. But this time, I turned to Jesus instead of my husband. We had to leave our beautiful four-bedroom, four-bathroom townhouse. It was during this time that I noticed the light in my husband's eyes had dimmed. A year or so passed in our new place, where we barely held onto our marriage. But our daughters were thriving, happy teens, and for that, I was grateful.

I was determined not to let my own internal issues damage my daughters' souls. I sought advice from other women and immersed myself in parenting lessons. The church I had been a part of for 18 years had taught me many things, and one of the most valuable was how to care for children's emotional needs. God is merciful to the humble.

But then, all hell broke loose. My husband lost his job, along with the company car and the Amex card. We hit rock bottom once again. And to add to the chaos, we found out we were expecting our first grandchild. For the second time, we had to move back in with my parents. My best friend during this time was the Holy Spirit. Remember, we were on the road to thriving!

Six months later—though it felt like an eternity—we saved enough money to get an apartment. This time, we had a new addition to our family: our beautiful granddaughter.

I learned to go beyond merely surviving and start thriving. I chose to be a spirit-led being rather than a religious one. Before this, I hadn't been growing in the fruits of the Spirit or displaying the image of God. I didn't truly know the Holy Spirit. In my blindness, I had become like a Pharisee—religious-minded but spiritually stagnant. Our lack of planning had given the enemy plenty of room to operate, trapping us in both financial and spiritual bondage. Yet, through it all, I remained faithful to the word marriage.

In this new church, I did a lot of spiritual work, which helped reveal my own heart. Both my husband and I carried baggage, disappointments, and past traumas. We needed restoration— neither of us was equipped to handle all the responsibilities that come with marriage and raising children. In hindsight, I realize I was more in love with the idea of being in love than with the reality of it. But finally, clarity began to emerge.

Then, everything shifted. Shock and confusion hit me when I lost my dream job working with the United States Tennis Association. It felt like a punch in the chest. Now, my husband had to carry the load alone. We found ourselves struggling again. But this time, I turned to Jesus instead of my husband. We had to leave our beautiful four-bedroom, four-bathroom townhouse. It was during this time that I noticed the light in my husband's eyes had dimmed. A year or so passed in our new place, where we barely held onto our marriage. But our daughters were thriving, happy teens, and for that, I was grateful.

I was determined not to let my own internal issues damage my daughters' souls. I sought advice from other women and immersed myself in parenting lessons. The church I had been a part of for 18 years had taught me many things, and one of the most valuable was how to care for children's emotional needs. God is merciful to the humble.

But then, all hell broke loose. My husband lost his job, along with the company car and the Amex card. We hit rock bottom once again. And to add to the chaos, we found out we were expecting our first grandchild. For the second time, we had to move back in with my parents. My best friend during this time was the Holy Spirit. Remember, we were on the road to thriving! Six months later—though it felt like an eternity—we saved enough money to get an apartment. This time, we had a new addition to our family: our beautiful granddaughter.

Our marriage was hanging on by a thread, held together only because neither of us wanted to be the first to say goodbye. It was like the Gladys Knight song—Neither One of Us (Wants to Be the First to Say Goodbye). That's exactly how we felt. After months of prayer and counseling, I saw the demonic cycle starting again, but this time, I allowed the Holy Spirit to guide me instead of my pride. My husband and I had the hardest conversation of our lives—a heart-to- heart. We both decided it was time to separate. I was on a journey of restoration, and he needed space for his own healing and restoration. For the first time, we both saw things clearly. We needed to get off this roller coaster.

My husband moved back up north, and it was just me, our adult daughters, and our granddaughter. At first, I felt a sense of resolve, but that quickly turned into anger. After all the sweat, tears, and pain, he really left! In those first few days, I called him, yelling out of fear and frustration. I remember walking around the college campus during my lunch break, filled with rage. The only way I knew to handle my fear was to remind him of all his wrongs. But thank God for prayer and the Holy Spirit. I stopped that destructive pattern and allowed my husband the space he needed to heal, in his own time.

The year was 2016. After four months of separation...

My husband said he wanted to save our marriage and was willing to get help. God moved in an unusual way. To this day, I'm not quite sure how I found Retrouvaille—a marriage ministry for couples in serious trouble, founded by the Catholic Church. We participated in a three-day marriage retreat that was fully paid for. It was truly a blessing. Interestingly enough, we weren't

Catholic, though my husband was a non- practicing Catholic when we first met.

Something surreal and supernatural took place during those three days. We spent our time on beautiful grounds, complete with a conference center and a stunning church nestled down a steep hill. We stayed in a cozy two-bedroom hotel-style room, and while the group sessions were intensive, they were exactly what we needed. My husband and I went in thinking we were the most loving couple there. But we soon realized that we had never been exposed to such deep betrayals and difficult situations—issues that made us question how people could be so cruel to each other. It was an eye-opener, and I realized I was the pot calling the kettle black.

The retreat was filled with testimonies from restored couples and guidance from professional clinicians. What made this experience unique was that for three full days, no one attending was required to speak. Instead, we were instructed to listen. Couples were even told not to interact with each other after the sessions. We would walk to our rooms or sit alone at tables. We were handed written exercises to complete individually, away from our spouses. This forced us to reflect on our own hearts and behaviors.

Eight years have passed since that retreat, and we are now best friends who truly enjoy spending time together. To stay connected, we visit different beaches in Florida every four months. We've come a long way—from surviving to thriving. Of course, life has continued to bring challenges over the past eight years.

We've experienced the deaths of my husband's mother, his surviving parent, as well as his sister. I lost my beloved daddy, my dear friend Shermone, my spiritual father, and even had to leave the church that had been instrumental in my spiritual growth. Friends I deeply loved have gone, and I made the difficult decision to step back from being an Independent Sales Director with Mary Kay. On top of all this, our grandson was born four months early during COVID, my youngest brother received a devastating health diagnosis, and I lost an aunt whom I adored. It's been a period of deep grief and many family concerns.

Despite these hardships, I've also experienced tremendous victories. Over the last four years, I've achieved emotional stability, something I lacked before. Our finances are now stable, and I have grown so much as a person. My husband is not my first love, but he is my true love—the kind of love that is grounded in agape, the selfless, unconditional love of Christ.

Dear friend, my prayer is that you can take a nugget or two from what I've shared. As Christians and disciples of Christ, many of us lack transparency and accountability for our actions, particularly in our marriages. Are you ready for my Beyond

Survival to Thriving in Marriage tips? The hardest part of this journey was being honest with myself. I had to look at the fruit of my actions and judge what I was producing in my marriage.

Here are my Beyond Survival to Thriving in Marriage tips—actions I wish I had taken sooner, or lessons I learned later as a wife:

- Get to Know Yourself
  Understand who you are in both good times and bad. Ask yourself, what is your biggest fear as a woman and wife? Here's a side note—why do you even want to get married? Knowing the "why" behind your desire for marriage is key to understanding yourself better.

- Study the Three Types of Love
  Do you know the difference between lust, friendship, and unconditional love? Before entering into marriage, it's important to explore the meanings of these three types of love:

    – Eros – Passionate, romantic love

    – Philia – Affectionate, friendship-based love

    – Agape – Selfless, unconditional love

- Ask yourself: Is your relationship built on mere attraction, or is it deep enough that you would walk through fire for your partner?

- DATE, DATE, DATE Each Other
Take the time to really get to know the person you're with. In my opinion, at least one year of dating is necessary before making any major decisions.

- During this time:
Take personality assessments. Understand your partner's personality, and respect it. Let him be who he is—don't try to change him.

- Read The 5 Love Languages by Gary Chapman.
It's crucial for building asuccessful relationship. My husband and I rushed things. We met in September, he moved to Florida in December, and we were married by July. We barely knew anything beyond "I miss you" and "I love you."

- Don't Compare Your Man to Someone Else's.
Every man is different! Avoid comparing your husband or partner to someone else's man. They are two completely different individuals, and comparisons only bring dissatisfaction.

- Check Your Alpha/Dominance at the Door.
When you come home, let go of the dominant, work-oriented mindset. You are a feminine woman—a wife and a mother. There are no deadlines or work assignments at home. The real work is learning to love and serve each other. Yes, it's a daily task, but trust me, the benefits are worth it.

- Set a Regular Time to Communicate Household Affairs. Make it a practice to ask your husband what day during the week or weekend works best for discussing household and family matters. This creates a rhythm for managing your home together. I also make it a point to ask my husband only one or two things in the morning to avoid overwhelming him.

- Know Jesus for Yourself.
  This might be the most important one. You cannot change anyone—only God can. Paraphrasing the scriptures: "Work out your own salvation with fear and trembling." Focus on your relationship with Christ first.

- Wisdom tip—make sure you have food in your house, that it's clean, and that your family's immediate needs are met before you go out serving others.

- Maintain boundaries in your marriage.
  Don't share all your business with your parents or girlfriends. Some matters should remain between you and your spouse.

- Husbands, cleave to your wife—not your mother.
  Wives, if your husband is overly attached to his mother, this is something that needs to be addressed immediately. Seek Godly counsel and use wisdom on how to communicate this with your spouse. Thank God, I never had to deal with this issue personally, but I know many couples who have.

MARRIAGE IS HONORABLE

KEREISIA BROWN-LYESAM

Achieving success while balancing relationships, faith, and career is far from simple. For me, it required first achieving personal wholeness, cultivating understanding through communication and support, setting both personal and relational goals, and prioritizing them. I also had to surround myself with a strong support system, commit to a realistic plan, remain adaptable, recharge, and avoid burnout.

I married at the age of 30. While some may argue that I married late, I have no regrets. Many of my family and friends were concerned that I was taking too long to find a partner because I spent so much time studying, traveling, and working, leaving little room for dating. When someone asked why it was taking me so long to marry, I once replied to a dear family member, "Do you expect me to stand on Highway 2000 with a sash that says, 'I need a man'? No. When the time is right, everything will fall into place."

I chose to wait, enjoying my life while working toward my goals. It's not that I never met anyone—I encountered many men, both clergy and non-clergy—but our goals either conflicted or didn't align. I was too focused on working hard to escape poverty and cross the finish line of success.

I was raised in a low-income household by my grandparents. My young parents struggled with financial hardship, relationship issues, and emotional trauma, leaving me in my grandparents' care as they tried to overcome life's challenges after raising eight children of their own.

My journey required me to first face life's challenges on my own before I could collaborate with someone else to achieve our shared goals. Throughout this journey, I developed various skills, a growth mindset, and strategies for success. I learned to be true to myself, set clear goals with strategies to achieve them, embrace lifelong learning, stay focused, and be confident, resilient, and strong. I also learned to be flexible, committed, adaptable, patient, and to prioritize self-care in the most cost-effective ways possible.

Now that I'm married, I can look back on those earlier difficulties and see them as a positive force. They helped prepare me to approach and overcome the challenges that inevitably arise in a marriage. Balancing my faith and career has been a process, and if I hadn't learned the skills mentioned earlier, I wouldn't have been able to face those challenges. These skills became the foundation that helped me navigate life's turbulent waters.

By the time I was ready to marry, my faith foundation was firmly laid, and I had earned significant educational credentials, including a Master's in Business Administration, a Bachelor's in Education in Food Service Production and Management, and a Teaching Diploma—all by the age of twenty-eight. I had also begun my professional career in a permanent position in Jamaica after working abroad in France and America. As a result, during my marriage, I could focus on blending my goals with my husband's, setting new shared goals for the growth of our family. Growing our family and achieving those goals did not come without its difficulties. We faced challenges such as witchcraft, jealousy, financial struggles, and health issues.

Individually, my husband and I have always been very goal-oriented. He began building a house at the age of nineteen and pursued a career in woodworking, farming, and owning a public passenger carrier business. He had to relocate to the city in search of better opportunities because his hard work was not yielding sufficient income. By that time, he already had two children and was eager to improve his financial situation to provide for them and achieve his personal goals. I met him while living in one of my deceased family member's homes. He had built a starter home, but when the chance for better opportunities in Kingston arose, he relocated, which is how our paths crossed.

God then opened the door to an even wider opportunity when my husband secured a job in Canada. This put us in a long-distance relationship for a while. When he returned, we got married. However, soon after our marriage, I had to leave my home due to family rivalry, and we relocated to my husband's house in a rural farming community. The area was surrounded by rivers, springs, and picturesque scenery, but it was far from the city, taking me about an hour and a half to commute to work.

We weren't fully prepared for the move, as there were still more opportunities in the city, but sometimes life's circumstances force you to strategize and manage your own affairs in unexpected ways. I quickly got used to living in this rural area even though it was three hours away from my hometown. It was cool and relaxing. However, I faced numerous challenges. The church leadership never accepted me because I wore pants and jewelry without a church hat. I truly understood how Jesus must have felt when He said, "I came to my own, and my own did not receive me." I had no family or friends in the community, and I had hoped to find comfort in my husband's church, since we served the same God. Instead, I was barred from participating in anything within the church and was criticized for not adhering to their practices, such as wearing certain clothes and attending their prayer meetings.

I felt frustrated and empty. But God, seeing my distress, led me to start a Community Bible Study and Prayer meeting, to help others understand His Word. He provided support through an elderly Christian lady, who generously allowed us to use her home for the sessions—something she had done in her more active years. Her warmth and cheerfulness created a welcoming atmosphere, and those who attended found refreshment in the Word. Through these Bible studies, I was introduced to a Bishop who needed a minister to manage his church while he was overseas.

God had been preparing me for this role for years. At 15, after accepting Jesus as my Lord and Savior, my pastor, inspired by God, sponsored my tuition to attend a one-year Bible school. It was an opportunity for me to deepen my understanding of the scriptures, even though I was the youngest in my class. My pastor recognized God's calling on my life and entrusted me with the microphone at a street meeting. Though timid at first, the Holy Spirit gave me such boldness that, by the end of my sermon, 23 men came to the altar. God is truly amazing.

That experience was part of God building my foundation in Christ. Serving the Lord as a youth gave me direction and purpose, shaping my character and transforming my mindset. In my home church, I served as a Lay Minister and Praise and Worship Moderator, helping the church fulfill its mission.

That strong foundation in Christ has been crucial in helping me balance my faith, career, and relationships.

One major challenge arose when we purchased a commuter bus for my husband's business, which initially brought in good profits. However, we soon faced a spiritual attack on our finances. All the money we had saved to buy a second bus ended up being spent on constant mechanical repairs for the first one. The situation worsened with accidents and the high cost of parts. Every penny we earned went toward fixing the bus, and eventually, we went bankrupt. We had to borrow money from friends and family, a burden that lasted until we finally sold the bus. Ironically, the person who bought it never had any issues with it.

I thank God for the help we received, though it brought significant financial strain and delayed the completion of our house. During this difficult time, I became pregnant after three years of marriage. However, I experienced severe hemorrhaging for three months before the pregnancy was confirmed. It was a frightening and unfamiliar situation for me.

One day, a friend called to intercede in prayer. She revealed that God had shown her there were enemies who wanted to harm me because I had helped my husband prosper so much. Concerned, I went to my gynecologist, but all the test results came back normal. Despite the reassurance, I continued to pass blood clots. My husband, ever supportive, would often accompany me to the bathroom during these distressing episodes. But through it all, I prayed constantly, leaning on my faith for strength.

One day, I had to leave work early because I felt extremely weak. While driving, I started to feel faint behind the steering wheel. I prayed fervently, declaring that I would not die but live to proclaim God's works, all while rubbing my numb face to stay conscious. I went to see my gynecologist that day, but she was not in the office. She agreed to let the nurse take me to the hospital, but I declined. My mother had dreamed that I would go to the hospital, lose so much blood that I would pass away. Unbeknownst to her, I was under a serious spiritual attack, but God was protecting me.

I visited six other gynecologists, but each time something prevented me from being seen—whether it was the health card machine not working, the doctor leaving, or simply not having enough money to pay. The last doctor I tried to see was a family friend, but the waiting room was so crowded with patients that I thought I might die before I was seen. On my way out, I slammed the brakes abruptly and, feeling death looming, I cried out, "Lord, this reminds me of the woman with the issue of blood. With the same power You have given me, I command this flow of blood to dry up in Jesus' name." I drove home, filled with faith.

God's power is so amazing that by the next day, not a single drop of blood remained. I need you to understand that God is truly powerful, and He will respond when you call upon Him.

Eight days after this miraculous event, I became pregnant. This was highly unusual. I didn't realize I was pregnant until four months later. When I checked the doctor's dates, I found that I had conceived just eight days after the blood flow stopped. It seemed impossible to me—how could I become pregnant after losing so much blood? It was nothing short of a miracle. Throughout the pregnancy, I experienced no further issues with blood flow. My blood pressure remained normal, and I had no more bleeding.

However, when I was admitted to the hospital to give birth, I found myself in a life-threatening situation due to errors made by both the nurse and the doctor. I was carrying a 10-pound baby, and although the doctors initially wanted to perform a C-section, the attending physician insisted that my birth canal was clear. The real issue arose when I was left unattended while the baby was coming down. By the time they transported me to the bed, the baby essentially jumped out. My womb tore, and it remained untreated for eight hours overnight. When the doctor finally arrived and began working on me without numbing the area, I screamed in agony, "Take me to the theater!" The pain was unbearable.

In the operating room, I nearly died, having lost three-quarters of my blood. I was close to death when a nurse touched me three times and said, "You cannot die now." I believe her words were deliberate, spoken with a purpose.

While I was still in the hospital, I had a dream. A dark angel visited me at my bedside. She was breathtakingly beautiful, with gleaming white teeth, and she said to me, "You see those eight doctors standing together? They want to kill you, but I'm going to take you out of here."

The next day, a nurse came over to check my blood pressure. She said, "I'm going to monitor your pressure constantly because it's time for you to leave the hospital." That same day, she discharged me. A doctor also came in and quietly confided, "I'll let you in on a secret: the dosage of medication you were receiving was incorrect." I felt that God was confirming the dream.

I was immensely grateful that the Lord had sent His angels to watch over me. That doctor, who closely monitored my condition, was a true blessing. After leaving the hospital, my doctor had to administer a blood substitute because I hadn't received the four units of blood initially prescribed. The doctors could only locate one unit in the entire country. Although I was gasping for air, I felt immense relief knowing that my baby was fine and I could care for him. Since then, I have had no further blood issues. I am thankful to be alive to share my story. During my recovery, my husband was incredibly dedicated to caring for me.

At one point, I was invited to become a minister for a new church. This role demanded a deep understanding, effective communication, and a genuine willingness to serve both God and the community according to His guidance. Balancing my responsibilities as a church minister, a manager at work, and caring for my husband and baby was challenging, especially with ongoing financial issues. I am deeply appreciative of my husband's support throughout this period.

He helped with household chores and church activities, demonstrating remarkable sacrifice to support both the church's growth and our personal life. Our focus was on serving others within the church and the broader community, organizing programs to address both physical and spiritual needs. Through God's help and our outreach efforts, we began to see a significant increase in community members attending church. Our aim was to illustrate God's love in a tangible way, showing that He desires our well-being—spiritually, emotionally, and physically. One of our notable projects involved building a house for a church member, ensuring his family could live comfortably, and providing school preparation classes for children in need.

My husband is an incredibly hardworking individual, but just before and during the COVID-19 pandemic, I found myself becoming the primary breadwinner. It was a challenging period, as managing loans and meeting our family's needs was incredibly tough. Every time we made progress, we seemed to regress due to financial difficulties. I am grateful for the support system of friends and family who stood by us and never turned us away. There were times when we hit rock bottom, struggling to pay our bills. Just as we resolved one problem, another would arise. Despite these struggles, God's support and the prayers of our friends were a constant source of strength. We faced financial attacks, with our money being targeted by malicious forces that seemed determined to create problems and steal from us.

In the midst of this, I found myself weary and my husband stressed. There were moments when I felt on the brink of losing my sanity, but I continued to speak life and God's word over my mind, bolstered by the prayers and counsel of our friends and family. I am truly thankful for their support and pray for God's blessings upon them.

I continued to support my husband in his business ventures. We agreed that expanding into the trucking industry would be a good move. Given my more stable financial situation, I took out a loan and purchased a truck, eventually growing our fleet from one to three trucks. God always provided, but as in the parable of the sower, challenges arose that threatened to undermine our progress. People often misconstrued our situation, assuming we were wealthy. One of the trucks was even given to us with the understanding that we would pay for it when possible, as the previous owner, a friend, was frustrated.

Despite facing obstacles, including jealousy and disagreements about building infrastructure for our trucks, we remained focused and determined not to give up. We believed that we would overcome these challenges and break free from the curses that seemed to plague our lives. Now, we are finally emerging from the wilderness and entering our promised land of abundance.

Though it took a long time for the prophecies of our deliverance from the dry places to come to fruition, we held steadfast to our faith, believing that faith is the substance of things hoped for and the evidence of things not seen. We are now witnessing the daily manifestation of God's promises. God is truly amazing.

At the same time, religious disputes arose over who would take over the church from me due to its significant growth. Seeing all I was enduring, the Lord instructed me to leave the community, much like Moses was directed. He told me to resign from the church and move to an unfamiliar place. I followed His command, trusting that when we obey God's instructions, He provides the resources needed to fulfill them. I felt disheartened, as my goal had always been to foster good relationships and use my knowledge and skills to support my husband's family.

God's guidance led us to a new beginning. We found a furnished home with affordable rent, and during the COVID-19 pandemic, we were blessed with the opportunity to purchase another piece of land with an incomplete house structure. Following God's instructions led us to our promised land, though it required selling one of our trucks to facilitate the purchase of the land.

Life was exceptionally challenging, as I faced jealousy and witchcraft aimed at hindering our success. Some believed my husband did not deserve a highly educated and virtuous wife, and this resentment created obstacles for us. Despite these difficulties, we persevered together. I remained committed to recognizing his potential, appreciating his skills as a singer, woodworker, farmer, and transportation driver.

For the past five years, my husband and I have had to adapt and switch roles due to the impact of COVID-19. He took on more responsibilities at home, caring for our baby, while I worked in a permanent position outside. We set clear objectives and collaborated to achieve them, supporting each other through every challenge.

Advice

- **Use God's Word as Your Compass for Faith, Relationships, and Career**

  God's Word, as outlined in the Bible, serves as a manual for every aspect of life. By reading and applying it, you can achieve success in your faith, relationships, and career. God's Word represents His voice and His thoughts about you.

Studying it allows you to receive guidance from the Holy Spirit. It contains the solutions you need. God knows the plans He has for you, including your spouse, and He has already orchestrated solutions for the challenges you will face. By tapping into His Word, you can receive direction for your life and navigate challenges effectively. As your Creator, God's principles are designed to guide you toward prosperity and good health. Following His Word will lead you to victory in all areas of your life.

- **Encourage Your Spouse's Goals and Set Goals Together Through Proper Communication**

Planning together is essential for creating a roadmap that prioritizes family goals and provides direction for growth. Both partners have unique personalities and aspirations, but it's crucial to work towards common goals that benefit the entire family. Communicate openly about your individual goals and the requirements needed to achieve them. Ensure your spouse is involved and can contribute, fostering inclusion and mutual support. Avoid risking all family resources on personal goals, as this can lead to disagreements, resentment, and lack of support. When your family understands your objectives, even if they lack experience in specific areas, they can provide meaningful support.

- **Be Patient and Supportive of Each Other**

  Achieving family goals requires teamwork. Be open to learning from each other and addressing gaps where one partner can offer expertise to help the other grow. Patience and support are vital for mutual development and success.

- **Don't Undermine Your Spouse's Weaknesses**

  Assess your relationship as you would a business SWOT analysis—identify and strengthen areas where your spouse may be weaker. Recognize each other's strengths and weaknesses and work to balance and enhance each other. Avoid agreeing with friends or family members who demean your spouse, even if you acknowledge their concerns. Focus on constructive support and growth.

- **Build a Strong Support System**

  At times, life can be stressful, and having a reliable support system is crucial. Relationships built on trust and mutual support can help overcome obstacles, solve problems, and maintain your relationship. No one can stand alone, and as God says, two become one.

  Relying on others for support can provide additional knowledge, resources, and wisdom to help you navigate challenges.

- **Take on the Role of Breadwinner if Necessary**

  Commitment is demonstrated through the traditional wedding vow: "...from this day forward, for better, for worse, for richer, for poorer, in sickness and in health, to love and cherish..." Life's challenges come in seasons, and they will pass. By praying, planning, working together, and remaining strong, you can overcome setbacks and support each other through difficult times.

MANAGING A DEMANDING CAREER, FAITH AND A RELATIONSHIP

KARLA STEPHENS-HALL

I am Karla—a wife, mother, daughter, corporate executive, transformational leader, and speaker. I mention being a daughter because, as women, we often feel it is our god-assigned duty to care for our parents when they cannot care for themselves. We may overlook this role in our list of responsibilities because it feels as natural as breathing.

The concept of balance is often used loosely, especially concerning wives and mothers. While we are nurturers for our families, many of us desire more. We may be multi-hyphenates with aspirations to add value and achieve great things through our passions, contributing to the world of business and beyond. This, combined with the responsibilities of motherhood and partnership, is a significant aspiration—but it CAN BE DONE!

Rather than using the term "balance," I prefer "manage" or "function effectively." Thriving amidst various demands involves understanding what needs to be done, organizing your life to accommodate these demands, prioritizing the important aspects at any given moment, and communicating with those who depend on you.

Navigating Marriage and Dreams

All life transitions can be challenging until you find the rhythm that best suits your circumstances and learn how to prioritize effectively. Transitioning from being single—where you are responsible and accountable only to yourself—to being married— a partnership where you are accountable to one another— while also building a career, has been an interesting journey for me.

As a natural go-getter who waits for no one, entering this new chapter of cohabitation and building a future with my husband required a shift. I had to figure out responsibilities and allow him to contribute in ways that made him feel valued in our shared life and well-being.

Navigating career goals, studying to advance professionally, and managing job responsibilities—especially when they require travel, sometimes for extended periods—can be particularly challenging for couples. This struggle is not uncommon, especially in an era where women are breaking traditional gender expectations. Many driven women will encounter these challenges at some point, which can lead to feelings of loneliness for both partners and potentially even infidelity.

Women may also experience guilt for not being able to nurture their relationships as much as they would like, due to their focus on other responsibilities when their partner may need them. It can feel as though taking a break from your goals is a sacrifice of yourself. Truthfully, prioritizing any aspect of life involves some degree of sacrifice. When you choose to spend time with your partner instead of studying or working, you are sacrificing one thing for another. It is essential to find a balance that maintains both your well-being and your relationships. Recognize that this balancing act is necessary for achieving both healthy relationships and career goals.

Our relationship endured this phase of life through deliberate actions and the setting of "couple" goals that aligned with our individual achievements and contributions. We approached this as a partnership by clearly communicating our goals, understanding each other's aspirations, and finding tangible ways to support one another. Transitioning from singledom to marriage meant being considerate of each other's wants and needs. Compromise and selflessness were sometimes required, and it was crucial to acknowledge and appreciate the sacrifices each of us made.

Selfishness would not have served us well, especially since achieving established goals would ultimately lead to the accomplishment of our shared partnership goals. It was necessary for me to overcome any personal inclinations and recognize the importance of mutual support.

Be sure to understand and communicate what makes both of you happy and manage each other's expectations in the relationship. If you find that you cannot meet these expectations or cannot reach a compromise, it may be a sign that this partnership is not right for you—don't be afraid to MOVE ON!!!!!

Partner Choice

Choosing the right partner is crucial if you decide that a relationship is important to you. When you have big dreams, have achieved some goals, and remain focused, it's essential to select someone who is not intimidated by your aspirations but instead becomes your biggest cheerleader. Look for a partner who is confident in his own identity and contributions to your emotional well-being. This kind of person will understand and support your growth and will be willing to make sacrifices to help you achieve your goals.

Marriage and Career Advancement

Balancing studying and career advancement can be challenging, but it's important to remember that the related stresses don't have to overwhelm your relationships at work or at home. While it's true that you can't completely leave work problems at the door or home issues at the parking lot—since all life experiences shape who you are and how you respond—it's possible to intentionally avoid letting them define your emotional state.

Home should be a sanctuary for happiness and connection. Therefore, it's crucial to compartmentalize some issues. Continuously bringing the weight of work and school stress into your home environment can create unnecessary tension, particularly if you're in a high-stress job or deep into professional development.

Mindset plays a significant role in transitioning from merely surviving to truly thriving in a busy life. I always sought to find my happy place in each situation. At work, if faced with stress, I approached challenges with a positive attitude and a smile, surrounding myself with individuals who radiated positive energy. At home, while I shared my work or study challenges, I made an effort not to let these discussions dominate our conversations. During my studies, I reminded myself of the saying, "If you want good, you nose haffi run," and pressed on, viewing each challenge as a learning experience. Remember too if you need your partner to "boost" your confidence in any area where you're struggling, let them know. They can't read your mind, so it's important to communicate your needs. ☺

Motherhood

When children come into the picture, you face a range of new and sometimes unexpected responsibilities, both emotionally and physically. Any parent will tell you that priorities shift significantly when caring for a child. Focusing on myself became much more challenging with the needs of my children to consider. I wanted to provide the absolute best for them and to mold and develop well- adjusted, good human beings for the world. But the demands they have are considerable.

Finding the "balance needed to thrive" involves prioritizing what is important for your experiences with your child and establishing a support system for times when you cannot be there. It's crucial to have someone reliable to step in when you absolutely cannot be present.

Mom-Guilt

The myth of being able to "do it all" often leads to a real phenomenon known as mom guilt. Many women, including myself, experience this as they strive to be the best mothers while managing the demands of their careers, passions, and other roles. I juggled being a mom, wife, company executive, and daughter of elderly parents, and I encountered mom guilt frequently:

During my maternity leave with my first child, I worked because I hadn't set up the necessary measures to disconnect from work.

Being new and under a specific time frame to complete key tasks, I often had my baby close by—either breastfeeding or beside me on the table. Despite this, I felt guilty for not being able to give her my undivided attention.

When I started my MBA while my second child was 2 years old, I did so to achieve one of my dreams and to be present for him as he began prep school. There were times when I was in online study groups, and it broke my heart to hear him cry for me while I needed to focus. Thankfully, my husband and good friends provided invaluable support during those times.

There were occasions when I came home, and my kids were already asleep, causing me to miss out on quality time with them after homework. My consolation was the quality time we had in the mornings. On the rare occasions when I managed to get home early, their elation was overwhelming because it was an unusual treat for them.

Despite these challenges, I never missed a graduation, school sports day, performance, or any other special school event. These were non-negotiables for me.

Understand that some decisions may require sacrifices that benefit you in the long run. Prioritize moments that make the sacrifice worthwhile. Now, when I put my kids to bed, I no longer have to study afterward, so our night-time routine has improved significantly.

Village

One of my secret weapons for overcoming mom guilt and ensuring my kids receive ample support was moving beyond the notion that I had to be the only one providing it. I engaged my support system, my "village," in a meaningful way. This village includes "aunties and uncles" who share in all the important milestones with my children, loving and caring for them as if they were their own.

If I can't attend an event, there's always a village member who can step in. This arrangement allows me to feel supported, and my kids know that there's always someone ready to step in for them, forming special bonds. They have an aunty for movies, an uncle for ice cream, another aunty who celebrates with gifts, and one who will be at every school concert, regardless of whether mom can make it.

Allowing people who want to be involved in your children's lives to participate in the ways they can is crucial. It's also important to coordinate with daddies or partners so that at least one of you is present for these milestones. Fortunately, my husband has a more flexible schedule than I do, so he takes on the role of swim and gymnastics dad. Our daughter knows her daddy is familiar with her routines and looks to him for support. Meanwhile, I make sure to spend quality time with her when I'm home, helping with reading and spelling, making tea, saying prayers, and putting her to bed when I can.

Being Intentional

After having my second child, I realized how crucial it was to be intentional about spending quality time with each child to meet their individual needs.

I made it a point to do school drop-offs some mornings, where we could have car conversations, discuss their interests, or simply sing and dance to music. Every moment, even the morning commute (and traffic), became an opportunity for quality time. I also structured my workday to include dedicated times when I could pick them up from school or be home to assist with homework and bond with them. Hearing them ask in the mornings, "Is it our day for pickup?" warms my heart, knowing they look forward to these moments of connection.

Don't forget about your partner. It's easy to let children and work consume all your time, but it's important to set aside intentional time for you and your partner alone. Whether it's going to a football match, watching TV, or taking a walk together, this time helps you connect, refuel, and strengthen your relationship. I admit this is something I struggle with the most, as kids often dominate your schedule, and you can easily get caught up in meeting their needs.

Setting Boundaries and Communicating

Setting boundaries and being transparent about my priorities was essential for managing all aspects of life effectively:

- I informed others that during specific times on certain days, I would be unavailable due to my daughter's activities or therapy unless the matter was urgent.

- I explained to my children that when I was working from home, that time was dedicated to focusing on work, so I could give them my full attention during designated quality time.

- When taking vacations with family or my spouse, I established clear "blackout" periods where no work was to be done, ensuring our focus was on bonding and enjoying each other's company.

- I made sure that everyone involved was aware of the purpose of my engagement in any activity at the time.

By setting, communicating, and being transparent with my boundaries, I fostered mutual respect for each other's time. This approach, combined with productivity and meeting deadlines, demonstrates your value and illustrates how prioritization enables task accomplishment.

Effective boundary setting and communication also reassure your family that despite the busy schedule, they are prioritized and will receive your undivided attention during designated times.

Women in Leadership

For women in leadership, setting boundaries is crucial, but effective delegation is equally important. To delegate confidently and efficiently, you must empower, coach, mentor, and foster the growth of your team members through succession planning techniques. This investment of your time is fundamental to balancing other aspects of your life.

Effective delegation ensures that when I was unavailable, my colleagues were empowered and confident to make decisions and execute tasks with minimal supervision. I dedicated time to delegating and coaching, focusing on enhancing my colleagues' and teammates' competence. This approach minimized the need for micromanagement, allowing me to oversee and review tasks for accuracy.

I also made it a priority to expose my direct reports to the information needed for their growth. This included sharing insights into my role, approach to issues, and problem-solving techniques. This strategy proved invaluable, as it ensured my staff were well-prepared and confident. Consequently, my team members were equipped to handle responsibilities effectively, even when my priorities shifted to other strategic work-related tasks or personal matters.

Self-Care and Mental Health

How many times have you heard, "You cannot pour from an empty cup"? Ladies, this is absolutely true. When you're mentally and physically exhausted, there's little energy left to love or pursue your passions. A multifaceted existence demands stamina and careful planning, but most importantly, it requires rest and rejuvenation. Sleep is crucial for revitalizing both mind and body, enabling you to face the world with renewed vigor.

Focusing on self-care and engaging in activities that help you regain your center is essential for maintaining a positive mindset and overall happiness. Without adequate rest, persistent fatigue can lead to increased anxiety, irritability, and a lack of interest in intimate interactions. This, in turn, affects your relationships with your children and others around you.

Burnout is a real risk and can occur if you don't recognize the signs of fatigue and take appropriate action. It's important to acknowledge when you need to pause and avoid taking on additional tasks that exceed your capacity. Learning to say "no" is a crucial skill for preserving your well-being.

Make time for activities that refresh you: exercise, take walks, get massages, go for a drive, or have some alone time doing what you love. Set aside regular date nights with your partner to maintain your connection. I admit that balancing these aspects is challenging for me, but I am determined to improve.

Additionally, dedicate time to pray and spiritually connect with God. This practice offers a sense of calm and reassurance, knowing there is a higher power looking after you and guiding your journey.

Functioning and Finding Balance

To thrive in all facets of life without succumbing to burnout, my advice revolves around having a clear understanding of your aspirations and the path to achieve them. Organizing yourself to reach both personal and professional goals requires prioritizing key activities that support your objectives.

Here's a summary of what you should remember:

- Embrace Your Multifaceted Life: You are fully justified in wanting to pursue a relationship, family, and a career. It's possible to have and excel in all these areas.

- Choose a Supportive Partner: Find a confident partner who is not threatened by your dreams or current achievements. Ideally, this person should understand the demands of the life you aspire to live and be willing to support you through challenges.

- Align Goals: Discuss and understand your partner's goals and how both of your aspirations fit together to create the life you want. Ensure that you are both on the same page and can support each other.

- Set and Communicate Priorities: Clearly define your priorities for different moments and communicate them effectively. This helps manage expectations and ensures that you can focus on what matters most.

- Be Intentional About Happiness: Organize your schedule around activities that align with your goals and provide fulfillment. Spend special, quality time with your children, even if brief. Every moment counts. Demonstrate to your kids that their events are a priority through your actions.

- Establish a routine where work or homework time is clearly designated, creating a sense of safety and consistency for your children.

- Make intentional time for your partner to ensure there is a sense of security amidst the chaos. Keep these moments sacred.

- Seek Help When Needed: Recognize that, despite your best efforts, you cannot do everything alone. Don't hesitate to seek support from your "village" when needed.

- Build a Reliable Structure: Cultivate a dependable support system. Coach and lead effectively to ensure that your team members are competent and can handle responsibilities in your absence.

- Prioritize Mental Health: Regularly take breaks to clear your mind and maintain your mental well-being. Your desire to live a full life and pursue your passions is achievable.

Use these tips to navigate the complexities of your life, understanding that sacrifices and compromises may be necessary. With determination and the right strategies, you can find balance and fulfillment in your journey.

Your desire to live a full life and harness your talents and passions is absolutely achievable. I encourage you to keep pursuing your goals and to use these tips to create a fulfilling and happy life. Remember, sacrifices and compromises are part of the journey, but with determination and the right approach, you will find balance and success. Keep moving forward, and trust that everything will work out well.

SECTION THREE

THRIVING IN
DIVORCE

MANAGING BUSINESS AND FAMILY AFTER DIVORCE

KAREN VAUGHN

Managing a Business and Family After Divorce: A Comprehensive Guide

Managing both a business and family life post-divorce can be a challenging endeavor. The overlap of personal and professional responsibilities becomes especially delicate when emotions run high during such a turbulent time. This guide offers insights and strategies on how to effectively manage both areas during this period.

1. Understanding the Emotional and Psychological Impact of Divorce

Divorce is more than just the legal dissolution of a marriage—it can trigger complex emotional responses. The end of a significant relationship often brings about a period of grief, much like experiencing a death. For example, I faced this kind of grief when the father of my child passed away when she was only 10 years old. I mourned the future I had envisioned, making it difficult to focus on daily activities, including my business responsibilities. Similarly, during my divorce after remarrying, I experienced anger and resentment, which fueled stress and conflict. These emotions can seep into your professional life, impacting relationships with colleagues and clients. Guilt and anxiety are also common during divorce. Many wonder if they could have done something differently to save the marriage, which can affect their decision-making abilities both personally and professionally. Recognizing these emotions and taking proactive steps toward healing, such as counseling and personal reflection, can be crucial for effectively managing your business and family life.

Emotional turbulence can lead to a lack of focus, poor decision-making, and burnout—affecting both personal and professional relationships.

2. Financial Implications

Divorce often brings about significant financial changes, and it's crucial to understand your new financial reality. As a business owner, I was faced with questions about how I could continue to support my business and maintain my lifestyle while navigating a new living situation. Scaling back and reassessing your business's financial health—cash flow, profits, and liabilities—

can be essential. A detailed post-divorce financial plan should include both personal and business finances.

This is where consulting a financial advisor can help. You may need to refinance debt, re-evaluate pricing strategies, or explore new revenue streams. Building a financial roadmap can prepare you for the challenges ahead and empower you to regain control over your financial situation, alleviating some of the stress that accompanies divorce.

3. Creating a Comprehensive Plan - Set Clear Goals

Setting clear goals is essential for managing both your business and family after a divorce. Whether it's stabilizing your finances, restructuring your business, or creating a nurturing environment for your children, defining specific and measurable goals will help guide your decisions. Reviewing these goals periodically will help you stay aligned with your evolving circumstances.

Delegate Responsibilities

Delegation is key to reducing stress in both your personal and professional life. At work, identify capable team members who can handle daily operations, allowing you to focus on strategic planning. At home, involve your children in age-appropriate chores, fostering teamwork and easing the post-divorce transition.

4. Communication is Key - Open Dialogue with Family

Honest and open communication is critical during a divorce, especially when children are involved. Transparent conversations can help alleviate confusion and provide reassurance to children. Using age-appropriate language ensures they understand the changes taking place. Encouraging them to share their thoughts and feelings creates a sense of security during a tumultuous time.

Professional Communication

At work, maintaining professionalism is crucial during personal upheaval. Keep workplace conversations focused on business, and implement regular progress reports to ensure that everyone remains aligned. Professional communication can help protect workplace relationships and maintain a sense of stability in the office.

5. Time Management Strategies - Establish a Routine

Creating a structured routine provides stability for both you and your family. Allocating specific time for work, family activities, and self-care will help you manage competing demands effectively. A well-defined routine fosters a sense of control during a chaotic period and helps you stay on track with your responsibilities.

Prioritize Tasks

Effective time management involves prioritizing tasks. Use tools like the Eisenhower Matrix to categorize tasks by urgency and importance. This framework allows you to focus on what truly matters, both in your business and family life, reducing overwhelm and enhancing productivity.

6. Self-Care and Mental Health - Importance of Self-Care

Self-care is crucial during a divorce. Regular exercise, a balanced diet, and sufficient sleep help maintain mental and physical health. Engaging in activities you enjoy, such as reading or spending time in nature, provides a much-needed mental break. Prioritizing self-care can enhance your resilience and help you navigate the challenges of divorce.

Seek Professional Support

Counseling or therapy can provide a safe space to express your emotions and develop healthy coping mechanisms. Group therapy or support groups can also foster a sense of community, reminding you that you are not alone. Seeking professional support is a proactive step toward healing and regaining control over your life.

7. Financial Management - Personal Budgeting

Creating a personal budget is essential to managing your finances post-divorce. By tracking your income and expenses, you can identify areas where adjustments are needed and ensure that you are living within your means.

Regularly reviewing your budget will help you adapt to changes in income and expenses.

Business Financial Health

Assessing your business's financial health is equally important. Evaluate cash flow, revenue streams, and expenses to identify areas for improvement. Making proactive adjustments, such as diversifying offerings or cutting costs, will help stabilize your business and position it for growth.

8. Teaching Children About Finances - Involve Children in Discussions

Including children in age-appropriate financial discussions helps them understand the changes taking place in the family. This fosters transparency and helps reduce their anxiety. Teaching children about money management at an early age equips them with valuable skills for the future.

Encourage Responsibility

Teaching children about budgeting, spending, and saving instills financial responsibility. Encouraging them to set savings goals helps them understand the value of money and fosters independence. These lessons will empower them to make informed financial decisions as they grow.

Conclusion

Managing a business while balancing family responsibilities post-divorce requires resilience, planning, and support. By setting clear goals, establishing routines, and prioritizing self-care, you can successfully navigate this challenging period. Open communication with family members and professional relationships will foster a sense of stability; while maintaining a disciplined schedule will help you focus on both your business and family. With determination and strategic planning, a fulfilling and balanced life is attainable.

LESSONS DIVORCE TEACHES US!

RHONDA SPENCER

One of the hardest things to do is pretend that our personal life does not affect our business life. Maybe some women can work through the chaos, but that wasn't the case for me. My name is Rhonda, and this is my story.

On June 24, 1989, at the age of 23, I got married. My Maid of Honor, who was my girlfriend, asked me if I loved him, and I told her, "No, but I'll eventually grow to love him." This statement was wishful thinking. I did grow to love him, but not the things he did or the decisions he made. God shows us warning signs, but sometimes we refuse to heed them. For me, it took longer to listen to the Holy Spirit. Although I was still in love with my ex- boyfriend, I married him anyway, believing I was ready for what life had in store.

I didn't fully grasp the importance of understanding my spouse's dreams and visions for the future. We were headed in different directions. I envisioned us wealthy, living in our dream home, doing ministry together, and owning businesses. I'm a driven woman, eager to travel and build a legacy for my children and grandchildren. But that wasn't his vision. Financially, we struggled because he was still trying to find himself at 24. He was unstable in his jobs, rarely staying for more than two years. As a result, I felt insecure in our marriage. I was the stable one, the head of the household—a role I resented.

Over time, I experienced several miscarriages, which, combined with the instability in our marriage, fueled my anxiety. In 2006, I helped my husband find a great job that paid for his education, and he excelled in it. I thought this would be the turning point for us. We made some progress, but then everything regressed. My husband began having issues in ministry, feeling underutilized, which led to a spirit of offense. He started exploring other doctrines online, which distanced him from both God and our family.

He began yelling at my son and me, claiming that God had told him to quit his job. When I asked about his plan, he had no answer. Without consulting me, he resigned from his job of over ten years and pretended he was still going to work each morning. He eventually stopped attending church and demanded that I stop as well to follow his new doctrine. He insisted that I must obey him as the head of the household, but I told him I would only follow him if he followed Christ. I knew I had to stand before God alone and could not follow my husband into something that contradicted God's Word.

This became mental abuse. For three years, we lived in the same house as roommates, in separate rooms. This was no longer a marriage. After 28 years of marriage, I looked back and realized I had only achieved one of my dreams—God blessed me with a handsome son whom I love deeply. However, the strain of my personal life clouded my mind, preventing me from being creative or physically pursuing my dreams.

In 2017, after our divorce, I hired a Life Coach who mentored both my son and me. My son was acting out at school, so I pulled him out and sent him to military school, where he thrived. Both of us needed counseling, and after numerous individual sessions, my coach recommended that I join a group. We met weekly and sometimes spontaneously, and through these sessions, I began to heal.

In 2018, I reconnected with my college sweetheart after thirty years. When we had dated in the past, our relationship was rocky due to his infidelity. This time, he apologized for his past behavior, but I was cautious. Despite my reservations, I forgave him, and we got married.

However, four years later, the glow I had once had dimmed. I found out that my husband had been cheating on me again. This time, the betrayal was even deeper. I had let my guard down, trusting that he had changed. I was wrong. He played games, took advantage of me, mentally abused me, and made me feel unworthy. The affection and romance were gone, and the other woman had control over my household. He even asked for my wedding ring back, showing a complete lack of respect.

I began experiencing health issues, fainting and dealing with unbearable stress. When I needed help, he wasn't there for me. Instead, I had to ask my son to take me to the hospital. These were distractions meant to derail me from my destiny. When your home life and self-worth are in disarray, your business goals suffer. My mind was too distracted to focus on my business.

I started my business, BeeSmart Educational Behavioral Consulting, LLC, in 2018 after I remarried. However, I struggled to get it off the ground. It felt like every door I tried to open was slammed shut. In a marriage, you and your partner must be aligned spiritually, financially, physically, and mentally. You need their support when embarking on a business journey. A lack of harmony in these areas will hinder your success.

After separating from my second husband, I faced a rollercoaster of emotions. I hadn't realized how spiritually and physically tied

I was to him. People hold onto marriages for various reasons, often not because of love, but convenience or finances. I now understand the concept of "soul ties." These are spiritual bonds created through intercourse that aren't easily broken.

It's crucial to create these bonds only within marriage, as they can be difficult to sever when things go wrong.

Fear is another obstacle—fear of being alone, of judgment, of failure. I had to cry out to God, praying and fasting for deliverance from my broken heart. And God did deliver me. I learned to let go of the old to make room for the new.

During my healing process, I sought counseling. My Life Coach, whom I had known for years, helped guide me through the trauma. In one of her group sessions, she discussed the traits of a narcissist, a personality disorder that I didn't realize applied to my own situation. Narcissists are people who have an inflated sense of their importance and lack empathy for others. When you leave a narcissist and go back to them, it reinforces their belief that you can't live without them, fueling their pride.

Once I left the toxic relationship, my husband's narcissism became even more evident. He treated me cruelly, but I refused to let him derail my life any longer. I focused on my spiritual well-being, and as I healed, God began opening doors for my business. He sent me destiny helpers who provided strategies for growth. He reconnected me with Dr. Joan Good, who recognized that I was pregnant with ideas and needed to give birth to books that had been inside me for years.

Don't be deceived—the state of your personal life absolutely affects your business life. I'm a living testimony of that truth. Now, I'm living my life to the fullest, with a healthy mind, body, and spirit, and my business is thriving.

I hope my story resonates with other women who may be going through similar struggles. Here are some practical steps I took to heal that may help you too:

- Seek help—talk to a therapist, pastor, or trusted friend.

- Face yourself and take responsibility for your part in the trauma.

- Spend quality time reading the Bible, fasting, and praying.

- Write down your goals and visions.

- Review your dreams and goals daily to stay focused.

- Eliminate distractions, whether they are situations, things, or people.

- Reflect on where you are and where you want to be.

- Take time to focus on yourself.

- Prioritize your life: God, yourself, family, job, etc.

- When overwhelmed, take a break and rest.

- Incorporate exercise or a hobby into your schedule.

- Surround yourself with positive people who uplift you and share your direction.

- Sharpen your spirit of discernment when making decisions.

- Focus on one task at a time and complete it fully.

- Manage your time wisely.

- Learn from your past mistakes but don't dwell on them.

- Learn to love yourself.

- Never give up, no matter how things may seem.

- Seek a second opinion when in doubt, from a reliable source.

- Prioritize the most important things in your life to stay on top of them.

YOU CAN SURVIVE DIVORCE AND THRIVE

ROSANNA BULLOCK

Dear Thriver,

For many of us, discovering what we were born to do involves recognizing the intersection of our passions, purpose, and unique strengths. It's about channeling our experiences, both joyful and painful, into something meaningful. That is the power our Creator has given us.

What do you feel called to do in this moment? How do your dreams and experiences shape the vision you hold for your future? Sometimes, answering these questions requires introspection and patience, but they can bring clarity and direction. I know this because I've gone through it myself. Reflecting on what I believe I was born to do has been a powerful exercise for me. I've done this self-assessment many times. Despite the pain and loss, my childhood dreams have remained a source of strength and inspiration. The fact that I've held onto them despite life's trials speaks volumes about the resilience and determination God has placed within me.

One of my most heartfelt messages to you would be, to take note of how loss can impact you at a young age. I've faced deep challenges and significant losses, especially the passing of my beloved grandmother. These experiences profoundly shaped my understanding of purpose and dreams.

My childhood, marked by strict discipline, secrets, loss, and faith, has guided me toward a purpose that not only honors my past but also transforms it into a source of light for others. I believe in the great calling God has placed on me—to share my story and help others navigate their challenges while pursuing a passion that brings healing and inspiration. Women of faith, you are called to do the same.

Exploring our purpose as women has led me to reflect on my own journey, which I feel compelled to share with you. Growing up without my biological mother, I was raised by my father's parents, my grandparents. At age 11, my grandmother passed away, and I continued to live with my grandfather and uncles while my father worked in other countries. During this time, I experienced and observed many things that sparked a significant dream within me.

At 11, I dreamt of marrying a devoted man of God. I envisioned a man who sought after God in all things and loved Him wholeheartedly. I believed such a man, fully devoted to God in prayer, worship, and submission, would also be devoted to his family. The Holy Spirit guided my thoughts, showing me what my future lifestyle could look like. One of my favorite Bible verses reminds us that while people look at the outward appearance, the Lord looks at the heart (1 Samuel 16:7).

A Journey of Faith: Embracing God's Love in an Imperfect Home

Growing up, daily family worship and active participation in church were integral parts of life and profoundly shaped my spiritual journey. Despite the imperfections of our Christian home, these experiences instilled in me a deep love for the Lord, which has only grown stronger with time.

Early Foundations in Faith

From a young age, family worship anchored my days. Each day began and ended with prayers and scripture readings, creating a rhythm that brought peace and purpose to our household. These moments, though simple, laid the foundation for a faith that would guide me through life's challenges.

Attending church was also a priority in my upbringing. Every Sunday, we gathered with our church community to worship, learn, and grow together. These gatherings were more than routine—they were opportunities to connect with others who shared our beliefs, reinforcing Christ's teachings in a collective setting.

Growing in Understanding and Love

As I grew older, my understanding of faith deepened. It became more than rituals or routines; it became a personal relationship with the Lord. I began to see how His teachings applied to my decisions and life circumstances. I remained dedicated to God and endeavored to serve Him more and more. After graduating high school, my aspirations grew—to use my gift of singing, create albums, and lead others to Christ while keeping myself encouraged.

Navigating Faith and Growth

Then, adulthood came. My young adult years brought new dreams and aspirations. Amid the confusion and dysfunction in my life, my spirituality began to waver, and I questioned everything I once believed—love, faith, and God. This was a pivotal moment, one in which I constantly asked: Who can I trust? What should I do next?

I embarked on a journey of self-discovery—seeking new experiences, connecting with different people, and exploring various spiritual practices, particularly praying and fasting. I realized that questioning my faith wasn't a sign of weakness but an opportunity for spiritual growth. It allowed me to reassess my values and redefine my beliefs.

Through this journey, I discovered that trust had to start within myself. By cultivating self-compassion and resilience, I found a renewed sense of purpose. My spirituality evolved into a more personal and encompassing understanding of love and faith.

Ultimately, this period of questioning led to a deeper connection with myself and the world. It reminded me that growth often comes from the most challenging times, and faith is found in the journey, not just the destination.

The Emotional Toll: Feeling Unheard and Unseen

As the months and years passed, the emotional toll of our relationship became more pronounced. The love we once shared was still there, but increasingly overshadowed by frustration, resentment, and loneliness. I began to feel unheard, unseen, and undervalued in our marriage.

There were times I tried to express my feelings and communicate the growing sense of dissatisfaction. But my attempts were often met with indifference or defensiveness. My husband would dismiss my concerns as trivial or shift the conversation to focus on his own needs and frustrations. This left me feeling even more isolated, as though my feelings didn't matter. I began to internalize these experiences, believing that perhaps I was the problem—that I was expecting too much or that my feelings were invalid. This self-doubt only deepened my emotional struggle, leading me to suppress my needs in an effort to maintain the peace and harmony I so desperately wanted.

Looking Ahead: The Road to Self-Discovery

These early years of marriage were a time of learning and growth, but also of struggle. The love and hope that once defined our relationship were tested by the realities of married life and unresolved issues that began to surface. As I navigated these challenges, I realized my understanding of marriage—and my role within it—needed to evolve.

The red flags, the dynamics that developed, and the emotional toll they took were all signals that something needed to change. I started to understand that maintaining peace at the cost of my own well-being was unsustainable. True harmony could only be achieved through mutual respect, open communication, and a willingness to confront the issues that were holding us back.

This realization marked the beginning of a journey of self-discovery—one that challenged my perceptions of marriage, my faith, and my own identity. It was a journey that ultimately led me to a deeper understanding of what it means to be a partner, a wife, and a woman of faith.

Educational Aspirations: Dreams Deferred

Throughout my marriage, one of my most enduring dreams was to further my education and complete my degree. From the earliest days, this aspiration was a source of personal fulfillment and a step toward achieving my professional goals. Education had always been important to me—not just as a means to an end, but as a way to grow, to challenge myself, and to better prepare for the future.

I remember the excitement I felt when I first expressed my desire to return to school to my husband. It was after the birth of our first child, a time when I was eager to carve out a path for myself beyond the roles of wife and mother. I expected support and encouragement, but instead, I was met with resistance. My husband quickly dismissed the idea, citing financial concerns and the demands of our growing family.

Though deflated, I convinced myself it was just a temporary setback. After all, starting a family was a big adjustment, and perhaps the timing wasn't right. So, I decided to put my educational goals on hold, believing the opportunity would come again when things settled down.

Years later, after the birth of our second child, the desire to return to school grew even stronger. While I cherished my role as a mother, I longed for something more— something just for me. I wanted to finish what I had started and prove to myself that I could achieve my goals despite the challenges of balancing family life. But when I brought it up again, the response was the same. My husband dismissed it, saying it wasn't in our budget. His words stung even more the second time, reinforcing a growing sense of frustration and helplessness. It wasn't just about the money; it was about feeling like my dreams didn't matter, that they would always take a backseat to everything else.

The final blow came when our children were in their early teens. After putting my educational goals on hold twice, I was determined to pursue them once more. But once again, I was met with the same resistance. My husband brushed off my ambitions as impractical, focusing on the financial strain it would place on our family. Each time I was denied the opportunity to pursue my education, it chipped away at my confidence and self-esteem. I began to believe that perhaps my dreams were too big, that they weren't worth pursuing. The more I was discouraged, the more I doubted my abilities and questioned whether I had what it took to succeed.

Emotional Isolation: The Cost of Unfulfilled Dreams

The repeated dismissal of my educational aspirations wasn't just about a lost opportunity; it was about the emotional isolation that followed. Each time I was told no, I felt more alone, more disconnected from my partner, and more uncertain about my place in the marriage.

What I longed for wasn't just the chance to return to school but the emotional support and encouragement that should have come with it. I wanted to hear words of affirmation, to know that my dreams were valued and that my partner believed in me. Instead, I felt like an outsider in my own life, as though my personal growth didn't matter as much as maintaining the status quo.

This emotional isolation extended beyond my educational goals, creating a sense of disconnection I couldn't ignore. I felt as though I was living a double life—presenting a strong, confident front to the world while internally struggling with feelings of inadequacy and unfulfillment. The lack of support from my husband made me question whether I was asking for too much, whether I was being selfish for wanting more out of life.

I struggled with feelings of guilt, wondering if my desire for personal growth was incompatible with being a good wife and mother. These internal conflicts only deepened my sense of isolation, as I felt increasingly unable to share my true thoughts and feelings with the person who was supposed to be my closest confidant.

As the challenges in our marriage grew more pronounced, I increasingly turned to my faith for comfort and guidance. I prayed constantly, asking God to help me navigate the emotional turmoil I was experiencing. I sought His wisdom on how to deal with the feelings of isolation, frustration, and disappointment that were becoming all too familiar. My faith became my lifeline, the one constant in a life otherwise filled with uncertainty. It was in these moments of prayer and reflection that I felt closest to God and began to hear His voice more clearly. The more I leaned into my faith, the more I felt that God was guiding me, helping me to see the path I needed to take.

Praying for Clarity: A New Approach to Spiritual Guidance

As the years passed, my prayers began to change. No longer was I simply asking for strength to endure; I was asking for clarity and direction. I began to pray for specific answers to the questions that weighed heavily on my heart. What was God's will for my life? How could I honor Him in my marriage, even when things seemed so difficult?

And most pressing of all, was there something I needed to change in myself or in my circumstances to truly thrive?

These prayers marked a shift in my spiritual journey. I was no longer content to merely endure; I wanted to understand. I needed to know what God was trying to teach me through these experiences, and I was determined to listen with an open heart. I asked God to reveal His will to me, to show me what I needed to do to find peace and fulfillment. One of the most significant changes in my prayer life came when I began to fast in conjunction with my prayers. Fasting, a practice I had turned to in the past, took on new significance. Through fasting, I sought to quiet the noise of the world and my thoughts, creating a space where I could hear God's voice more clearly. It was during these times of fasting and prayer that I felt God's presence most profoundly, and through these practices, I began to receive the answers I had been seeking.

Encountering Resistance: The Struggle to Seek Help

While my faith provided me with spiritual guidance, I also recognized the importance of seeking help from others—particularly in the form of counseling. I believed that counseling could offer a space where my husband and I could work through our issues with the guidance of a neutral third party, someone who could help us see things from a different perspective and facilitate the difficult conversations we needed to have.

However, each time I brought up the idea of counseling, I was met with resistance. My husband viewed counseling as unnecessary, a violation of our privacy, or even as an admission of failure. He saw no need to involve a third party in our relationship, and his reactions made it clear that he was uncomfortable with the idea of discussing our problems with someone else.

The resistance was not just verbal; it manifested in actions as well. On several occasions, after I had arranged for counseling sessions, my husband would react with anger or frustration. There were times when he would slam the car door or make comments that left me feeling guilty for even suggesting counseling. These reactions made it clear that he was not open to the idea, leaving me feeling even more isolated and unsupported.

Despite his resistance, I knew that counseling was something I needed, even if it meant going alone. On three different occasions, I attended counseling sessions by myself, hoping to gain some insight into our relationship and find a way to move forward.

While these sessions were helpful in some ways, they also highlighted the deep disconnect between my husband and me. It became clear that without his participation, counseling could only go so far in addressing the issues we faced.

A Profound Revelation: God's Voice in the Silence

During one of my periods of fasting and prayer, I had a profound experience that would change the course of my life. It was in the early morning hours, a time when I often found myself awake, reflecting on my life and my prayers. On this particular morning, I felt an overwhelming sense of peace, and in that peace, I heard a voice—a voice that I believe was God speaking directly to my heart.

The message was clear: "You cannot thrive where you are." These words echoed in my mind, resonating with a truth I had been avoiding for so long. For years, I had been trying to make the best of my situation, to find a way to thrive within the constraints of my marriage and the emotional challenges I faced. But in that moment, I realized that true thriving wasn't possible in an environment that stifled my growth and left me feeling isolated.

This revelation was both comforting and terrifying. On one hand, it confirmed what I had been feeling for so long—that something needed to change. On the other hand, it meant making some difficult decisions about my life and my marriage. I couldn't continue to live in a way that was incompatible with the person God was calling me to be.

Understanding "Unequally Yoked": A New Perspective

One of the most significant insights I gained from this period of spiritual reflection was a deeper understanding of the concept of being "unequally yoked." Growing up, I had always understood this phrase to mean marrying someone who didn't share the same religious beliefs. But through my prayers and reflections, I began to see that it went deeper than that.

Being unequally yoked, I realized, wasn't just about differing religious beliefs; it was about a fundamental disconnect in values, priorities, and spiritual engagement. It was about being in a relationship where one person was spiritually invested and the other was not, where one person sought growth, and the other was content with stagnation. This realization was both painful and liberating, as it gave me the clarity I needed to understand the challenges I was facing in my marriage. With this new perspective, I began to see my marriage in a different light. I understood that the struggles we were facing were not just about personality differences or communication issues; they were rooted in a deeper spiritual disconnect. This insight helped me to make sense of the feelings of isolation and frustration that had plagued me for so long and provided a framework for understanding the changes I needed to make in my life.

Understanding Unequally Yoked: A Deeper Insight

For much of my life, I had understood the concept of being "unequally yoked" in the context of religious beliefs. It was a phrase I had heard often, one that conjured images of couples struggling to find common ground because they belonged to different faiths or held different religious views. I had always assumed that because my husband and I shared the same religion, we were equally yoked. But as the years went by, and as I delved deeper into my faith, I began to see this concept in a new light.

Through prayer, reflection, and the guidance of the Holy Spirit, I came to realize that being unequally yoked wasn't just about religious labels; it was about the depth of spiritual connection, shared values, and the willingness to grow together in faith. It was about being aligned not just in belief, but in practice, purpose, and the way we sought to live out our faith in everyday life.

This realization hit me hard. I began to see that while my husband and I shared the same religious background, our spiritual journeys had taken us in different directions. I was seeking a deeper relationship with God, one that required constant growth, reflection, and commitment. I was striving to align my life with God's will, to listen to His voice, and to follow His guidance. My husband, on the other hand, seemed content with where he was, with little interest in deepening his spiritual walk or engaging in the practices that had become so important to me. This disconnect became increasingly apparent in the way we approached life's challenges. When faced with difficulties, I turned to prayer, fasting, and seeking God's guidance. My husband, however, often retreated into himself, avoiding the spiritual work that I believed was necessary to navigate the complexities of life. This disparity in our spiritual engagement left me feeling isolated, as though I was carrying the weight of our spiritual life on my own.

The Revelation: A Moment of Clarity

The moment of revelation came during one of my periods of intense prayer and fasting. I had been struggling with the sense that something was deeply wrong in our marriage, but I couldn't quite put my finger on it. I prayed fervently, asking God to show me what I needed to see, to reveal the truth hidden beneath the surface. One early morning, as I sat in quiet reflection, I felt a profound sense of peace wash over me. It was as if the answers I had been seeking were finally within reach. In that moment, I heard a voice— clear, calm, and unmistakable: "You are unequally yoked." These words echoed in my mind, resonating with a truth I had been reluctant to face.

The realization was both shocking and liberating. For years, I had been trying to make sense of the disconnect in our marriage, the sense that we were growing apart rather than together. I had attributed it to various factors—communication issues, personality and external stressors—but now I saw that the root of the problem was spiritual. We were not on the same path, not seeking the same things, not growing in the same direction. And this spiritual mismatch was the source of the tension, frustration, and emotional isolation I had been feeling for so long.

A Turning Point: Embracing the Truth

This revelation marked a turning point in my life and marriage. It was as if a veil had been lifted, allowing me to see clearly for the first time. I could no longer ignore the reality that we were unequally yoked, and this disconnect was preventing us from truly thriving as a couple.

With this new understanding came a sense of urgency. I knew that something had to change, that I couldn't continue to live in a way that was incompatible with the person God was calling me to be. I had to confront the reality of our situation and make the necessary changes to align my life with God's will. It was a painful but necessary step, one that required courage and faith. In the days and weeks that followed, I began to take concrete steps to address the issues in my marriage. I continued to seek God's guidance, praying for wisdom and strength as I navigated the difficult conversations and decisions that lay ahead. I sought out support from trusted friends and mentors, individuals who could offer perspective and encouragement as I worked through the challenges.

Finding Peace: A Journey of Healing

As I began to confront the reality of being unequally yoked, I found a new sense of peace. It was a peace that came not from resolving all of my problems but from accepting the truth and trusting that God was guiding me through this difficult period. I knew that no matter what the future held, I was walking in faith, seeking God's will, and doing my best to honor Him in all aspects of my life. This journey of understanding and healing has been transformative, leading me to a deeper relationship with God and a greater sense of clarity about my own path. It has taught me that while the road may be difficult, trusting in God's guidance and embracing the truth is the key to finding peace and fulfillment in every area of life.

This often meant making sacrifices—swallowing my own feelings, avoiding difficult conversations, and putting on a brave face even when I was hurting inside. I believed that by keeping the peace, I could somehow protect my children from the emotional fallout of our marital struggles. But deep down, I knew this approach had its limits.

Despite my best efforts, it was clear that my children were still affected by the tension in our home. They began to show signs of stress—withdrawal, mood swings, and a reluctance to engage in family activities they once enjoyed. I tried to reassure them with extra love and support, but I could tell they were grappling with feelings they didn't fully understand. One of the most difficult aspects of this period was realizing that my attempts to protect my children weren't entirely successful. I had hoped that by maintaining a calm exterior, I could shield them from dysfunction, but it became evident that they were absorbing more than I had anticipated. The emotional strain in our home was impossible to fully conceal, and I began to worry about the long-term effects this might have on their well-being.

Facing the Reality: Acknowledging the Impact on the Children

As months and years went by, I had to confront the reality that my children were being affected by the unresolved issues in our marriage. It was no longer enough to simply keep the peace; I needed to address the deeper issues causing this dysfunction. I knew that if I didn't take action, the emotional toll on my children could become even more significant.

I began having more open and honest conversations with them about what was happening in our family. I didn't want to burden them with details they were too young to understand, but I also didn't want to pretend that everything was fine when it wasn't. I tried to strike a balance between being truthful and protective, reassuring them that despite the challenges we were facing, they were loved and supported.

These conversations were difficult, but necessary. I wanted my children to know that their feelings were valid and that it was okay to be confused or upset about what was happening. I also wanted them to understand that the issues between their father and me were not their fault, and that we were doing our best to work through them.

Healing and Rebuilding: Steps Toward Family Restoration

Recognizing the impact of our marital struggles on our children was a turning point for me. I knew that I couldn't continue to let them live in an environment where tension and emotional distance were the norm. I needed to take active steps toward healing and rebuilding our family dynamic.

One of the first steps was seeking professional counseling. While my husband had resisted it in the past, I felt it was crucial for our children to have a safe space to express their feelings and receive support. I arranged individual counseling sessions for myself, as my spouse continued to resist. I also suggested and arranged individual sessions for our children and family counseling sessions where we could begin to address the issues affecting us as a unit.

These counseling sessions were transformative for me. When my spouse attended two of the sessions, he acknowledged that they were helpful. The sessions were meant to provide a space for open dialogue, where my children could voice their concerns and fears without feeling judged or dismissed. Though I hoped the sessions would mark the beginning of healthier communication as a family, they did not bring about the change I anticipated.

In addition to counseling, I made a conscious effort to prioritize quality time with my children. I wanted to create positive memories and reinforce the bond we shared, even amidst our challenges. We spent more time together as a family, engaging in activities that everyone enjoyed. A particularly special moment was when I arranged their first plane ride, taking them to New York. This trip allowed them to visit their parents' homeland and experience a new adventure together. During these moments, I made sure to be fully present, cherishing the time we spent as a family. I also focused on creating a spiritually nurturing environment at home. I encouraged mindfulness through prayer and devotion, guiding them to seek comfort and guidance from God. My hope was that this would strengthen their faith while providing stability and reassurance during uncertain times.

Trusting God with the Process: Faith as the Foundation of Healing

Throughout this journey, I leaned heavily on my faith, trusting that God was guiding us through this difficult time. I prayed constantly for wisdom, strength, and healing— not just for myself, but for my entire family. I believed that God had a plan for us, even if I couldn't see it clearly in the moment.

One scripture that brought me comfort during this time was Exodus 14:14: "The Lord will fight for you; you need only to be still." This verse reminded me that even when I felt powerless, God was at work in our lives, fighting on our behalf. It gave me the strength to keep going, to continue seeking healing for my family, and to trust that we would come out stronger on the other side. I also found solace in knowing that healing is a process that takes time and patience. I knew our family dynamic wouldn't change overnight, but I was committed to doing the work necessary to create a healthier, more loving environment for my children. I continued to pray for guidance, asking God to show me the steps I needed to take and give me the courage to follow through. Over time, I began to see positive changes in our family. The tension in our home started to ease, and the emotional distance that once defined our relationships began to close.

My children became more open and communicative, and I felt a renewed sense of connection with them. While our journey was far from over, I was encouraged by the progress we were making.

A New Chapter: Moving Forward with Hope

As I reflect on this period of our lives, I see it as a turning point—a time when we began to move from dysfunction and pain to healing and restoration. It wasn't an easy journey, but it brought us closer as a family and strengthened our faith in God's ability to heal even the deepest wounds. Now, I look forward to the future with renewed hope. Challenges will continue to arise, but I am confident that we have the tools and the faith to navigate them together. My children are growing into strong, resilient individuals, and I am committed to supporting them as they navigate their own journeys.

This experience has taught me that healing is possible, even in the most difficult circumstances. It has reinforced the importance of addressing issues proactively, rather than letting them fester and affect those we love. Above all, it has reminded me that with faith, love, and perseverance, we can overcome even the most challenging situations and emerge stronger on the other side.

But fortified in faith, I knew it was time to rise and fight for the preservation of life— life that God had promised me. It was a call to honor the vision I had dreamt of, one that the Holy Spirit affirmed. Though the path ahead was both clear and frightening, I understood that it was time to stop living for others and begin embracing the transformation God desired for me. There have been countless defining moments that cast a dark shadow over my life and the lives of my family. Too many to recount in one chapter. Yet, one moment stands out clearly—the summer of 2018. At that time, I had dedicated myself to fasting and prayer for my son, seeking clarity and divine intervention. After seven days of fervent prayer, my son approached me, asking to speak. I could sense the weight of something significant in his voice.

"Mom, sometimes I feel like I'm walking, and all I see is fog," he said.

His words hit me with a force I hadn't anticipated. My heart sank, but in that sinking came a powerful surge of gratitude. I cried out, "Thank you, Lord!" I believed God had answered my prayer, revealing the very struggle I had discerned in my son.

Overcome with emotion, I embraced him tightly and immediately knelt in prayer, thanking God for His mighty covering over my son. That moment was filled with tears and overwhelming emotion—a shared pain and hope between us. From that day forward, I have never ceased pleading the blood over my children, trusting in divine protection and guidance. For too long, I allowed everyone in my family to cross boundaries in their treatment of me—a treatment I did not deserve. By doing so, I unintentionally gave them power over me, leading to a growing disregard for my feelings. My children came and went as they pleased, ignoring any input I had.

It felt as though nothing I said mattered. Every day, I looked at myself and felt belittled, as if my voice had been stripped away. I feared the strange looks. I felt uncomfortable in my own space. I couldn't express myself, and there was no one to speak on my behalf. I kept asking, where is the priest of this home? I couldn't stay in an environment where I felt invisible and lonely, even though I was surrounded by people.

Among the many instances that stand out, I remember when my prayer group at work and I held a prayer and fasting session. We bought extra virgin olive oil, prayed over the bottles, and agreed to anoint certain areas of our homes and our children's doors. When this was discovered at home, the marks on the door were noticed, and I was laughed at and questioned about why I had done such a thing. The mocking comments that followed left me feeling humiliated. I had no human defense, but God was ever-present with me. For thirty years, I prayed for unity within my marriage, but no change ever came. When Covid-19 struck, it felt like a savior amidst the turmoil, offering clarity. I resolved to separate from my marriage after years of emotional exhaustion.

This decision, long in the making, felt like a healing touch from God. God showed me that perfect love drives out fear (1 John 4:18), and He helped me accept that I wouldn't be alone. He reassured me with His promise: "I will not leave you as orphans; I will come to you" (John 14:18). This journey felt like reliving my childhood, where the shadow of abandonment once loomed over me. But God gave me the confidence to move forward. As I sought Him first, He delivered me from my fears (Psalm 34:4), silencing the lingering thoughts about what others might say. Their opinions no longer mattered. God reminded me that I can do all things through Him who strengthens me (Philippians 4:13).

Attitude is a Habit of Thought

Attitude has always played a significant role in my life. It's more than just a mindset; it's a habit of thought that shapes every decision, every action. For me, attitude is about living with love, finding joy in laughter, embracing gratitude, maintaining inner peace, showing compassion, pursuing meaningful goals, and living with purpose. It's about serving in the work of the Lord, seeking continuous self-development, and surrounding myself with positive, like-minded people.

In March 2020, this habit of thought became more crucial than ever. It was an early Saturday morning. My spouse had left for work, and the house was quiet—my son living elsewhere and my daughter away for the weekend. Alone with my thoughts, I reflected on the years, months, and days that had led me to this moment. My heart was weary, burdened by all that had transpired, and I knew the time had come to make a change.

I began packing my personal belongings—clothes, shoes, books—gathering the pieces of my life that I wanted to take with me. In past conversations, I had often said that if I ever left, I would only take what held memories of my children: photos, mementos— those things that mattered most. And so, I did just that. I left behind everything else, taking only those precious memories with me. This decision was not made lightly. It reflected my habit of thought—a culmination of years of living with intention, guided by principles that have always been important to me. It was a step towards living a life aligned with my true self, one rooted in love, laughter, gratitude, peace, and purpose.

Now that I'm gone, the sting of failure hits me again. But deep down, I know that each day mattered. God called me out of darkness into His marvelous light, as 1 Peter 2:9 reminds me. He called me out because He had a greater purpose for my life, a "me" He wanted me to discover. His plans were different from what I had planned or expected.

"I matter too much to God not to enjoy the precious joys He has for me. Life is too short to live in worry because my soul is too precious to waste on things that don't add value to this world. Most importantly, God is too good for me to place my attention on people and things that care nothing about me." **Soul Speakers**

As time passed, I would occasionally see my daughter. I continued buying groceries and dropping them off for both her and my spouse. But once again, my acts of kindness were taken for granted. In one counseling session, I tearfully shared how I felt used. The counselor told me that I was an enabler and needed to stop enabling others. Reflecting on that advice, I knew I had to put an abrupt end to what I was doing during my separation.

In Iyanla Vanzant's book Living Through the Meantime, she asks, "Where is the mess?" She then says, "A feeling is the energy that moves you in one direction or another." My feelings were indeed moving me in a new direction. In the "basement" chapter of her book, she says, "Today you will begin to realize that the only relationship that matters is the one you have with you. Today you will begin building a new, improved relationship." Wow—powerful words! I was in the basement of my life, and this was a bold, bright light that illuminated it. This alone time became a sacred moment between me and God.

Five months after I left, I moved to a new city. As I settled in, I felt increasingly overcome by the power of the Holy Spirit. God began speaking to me more frequently through His Word. It was astonishing how the same Bible verses seemed to appear everywhere I turned—whether in my personal devotions, church sermons, online devotions, teachings from various preachers, or prayer groups. God used every avenue to communicate with me. Then, I heard Him say, "Be still, and know that I am God" (Psalm 46:10). In my quietness and confidence, I found strength. Filled with the wisdom of God's Word, as Colossians 3:16 says, I decided the following summer— sixteen months after I left, in July 2021—to file for divorce. I remembered a preacher once said, "Bad selection worsens the situation," and "We must declutter for clarity so we can find ourselves. We get lost amongst all the clutter." How true that was! There was nothing to divide in the divorce, and I had already made it clear in past conversations that I didn't want any of the house contents. So, without involving lawyers, I handled everything on my own.

By January 12th, the papers were signed. The following month, as I officially became a divorcee, I would also divorce and bury my old self, along with the sins of my past, and rededicate my life to God. One month later, on February 12th, I was rebaptized. Today, I am living by faith. The enemy tried to attack again, using the same tactics as before to target my mind and heart. But I had learned from past experiences and decided, "No more." I know who I am. God knows who I am, and He had shown me what to do once again. So, I took charge. This is when I learned the importance of boundaries. I hadn't set boundaries before, and it was time to develop them. After all, Jesus set boundaries for Himself that were in line with His values and mission (Mark 1:38). Why should it be any different for me—or for you, dear Thriver?

It's not enough to simply understand our needs; we must also ensure those needs are met. As I gained a better understanding of boundaries, I began identifying new symptoms, conflicts, and the underlying needs driving those conflicts. Most importantly, I started putting boundary skills into practice, as described in the book Boundaries by Dr. Henry Cloud and Dr. John Townsend.

Everything I hoped for seemed to unravel in the opposite direction. It became clear—I was being pushed down when I desperately needed support. Those I once relied on turned their backs on me, leaving me feeling rejected, too fearful to engage in conversations, no matter how hard I tried. Wrong was being celebrated as right, and lies spread like wildfire. It felt as though I was reliving past pains all over again.

I came to understand that the enemy of our souls customizes his attacks, knowing our weaknesses intimately. As I began to recognize these patterns and the enemy's schemes, along with my newfound understanding of boundaries, I realized it was time to move forward once more. God opened a path for me to be completely alone—a time meant for private, uninterrupted communion with Him, a chance to serve Him wholeheartedly and worship Him one-on-one.

In this solitude, God reminded me of His promise in Romans 8:28: that for those who love Him and are called according to His purpose, He will work all things together for good. He showed me that He wanted me to be surrounded by like-minded people who respect and appreciate me. Admittedly, this last trial was the hardest for me to endure.

Indeed, looking back is not an option for none of us. The future shines brightly, as the Lord assures me in Psalm 16:6-11. I have lived and continue to embody some of the attributes of the Proverbs 31 woman. I have worked hard all my life, and now, I am learning to work smarter. Armand Nicholi once said, "Time is like oxygen—there's a minimum amount that's necessary for survival. And it takes quantity as well as quality to develop warm and caring relationships." I thank God for the wonderful relationships that have developed in my life. While I value quality over quantity, I am grateful for the abundance of meaningful connections I've made over time.

These relationships have been my rock through the years, and for them, I am truly thankful.

The time is now, in my latter years, to live a wholesome and victorious life. I sometimes tearfully reflect on the words of my firstborn, my daughter, who said, "Mom, live your best life, whatever it looks like." Her words propelled me forward because I have always wanted my best life to be an example for her and my son. My prayers and wishes for them remain the same every day.

As I continue to embrace this wholesome and victorious life, I reflect often on my daughter's poignant words: "Mom, live your best life, whatever it looks like." Her encouragement has been a guiding light, reminding me to aspire to a life that serves as a powerful example for both her and my son. Every day, my prayers and hopes for them remain steadfast.

In her book **You Are Different for a Reason - Maximize Your Difference**, Dr. Joan Wright writes, *"When you are committed to something, you accept no excuses, only results. So, stay on the path and don't look back. If you look back too much, you'll be heading that way sooner than later. Forget where you have been and start looking at where you can be because your destiny and call in life is always forward, never backward. Never forget or look back unless you are regretting and repenting sin."*

Indeed, looking back is not an option for any of us. The future shines brightly, as the Lord assures me in Psalm 16:6-11. I have lived and continue to embody some of the attributes of the

Proverbs 31 woman. I have worked hard all my life and am now learning to work smarter.

Each day matters. I am an overcomer—forgiven, a forgiver, and a child of God called to serve and inspire. I am loved and, despite being battle-tested, I am God's masterpiece, created in His image, even in my brokenness. I am not just a survivor; I am a thriver!

Who are you on this journey of life, Beloved Reader? Do you ever feel powerless? Are you enduring a season of brokenness, burdened by pain that feels insurmountable? Does the light at the end of the tunnel seem out of reach?

Take heart! You are more resilient than you know. You are a Thriver. You are Fearless. Trust in the One who created you and walks beside you, even in your darkest moments. Remember, the shadow of a dog cannot bite you—similarly, the shadow of your enemy is just that, a shadow. Stay anchored in Jesus, for He is your light and your strength.

As you continue on this journey, remember to love deeply, forgive freely, and live with a heart full of gratitude. Be driven by your purpose, believe in yourself, and govern your attitude with grace. Embrace joy, seek peace, find rest, and most importantly, keep thriving.

Sincerely yours in service,

Rosanna, CCP, DTM

Soul Speakers CEO – Be Soulful. Be Dynamic.

*"Trust in the Lord with all your heart
and lean not on your own understanding."
– Proverbs 3:5(NIV)*

THE MOMENT OF REALIZATION

DR. SHALETTE ASHMAN

I realized that things were not going well in my marriage. It wasn't a sudden epiphany but rather a gradual unveiling of truths I could no longer ignore. My husband and I had spent our 20s, 30s, and mid-40s together, building a life that, from the outside, seemed great. We started with nothing, both driven and ambitious, and I believed wholeheartedly that we could create a life together. Our shared dreams were big—building a future and perhaps having children. But over time, those dreams began to fade, replaced by a cold, stark reality.

At first, there were subtle signs, like shadows creeping into the corners of our relationship, dimming the light that once shone so brightly between us. Our conversations became limited, with most questions answered in monosyllables, as if engaging in dialogue required too much effort. Eventually, I felt like I was living with a stranger—the man who had once been my partner in everything now seemed like a distant presence in our home.

I tried to ignore it, to push through the discomfort, convincing myself that it was just a phase and that things would get better. But the signs kept piling up, each one a small betrayal of the life we had built. I felt he didn't appreciate the little things I did for him. For instance, when I prepared his meals, he refused to say thank you, yet he always expressed gratitude when our helper did. This behavior was particularly upsetting. It felt like a knife to the heart, a painful reminder of the growing distance between us. I started to feel invisible in my own home, my efforts unnoticed, my love unreciprocated.

The most glaring moment came after I underwent a myomectomy, a procedure that left me in significant pain. I will never forget being driven home, feeling like an animal, with the car hitting every pothole. In that moment, I felt more like an inconvenience than someone recovering from surgery. I winced with every jolt, pain shooting through my body, and when I asked for a more careful drive, my pleas were dismissed as an annoyance. To make matters worse, despite living in the same country, only my family showed any concern for me after the surgery.

While I was venting in our bedroom about the lack of concern from his family, my words were secretly recorded and later played for his mother. It felt like a deep betrayal to have my private frustrations in my own home used against me in such a way.

In contrast, a friend of ours who came to Jamaica to stay with us for a myomectomy received the utmost care after her surgery. When she was driven home, every bump and pothole was carefully avoided. She was even given a warning about the upcoming rough road so she could prepare herself for the ride. Watching her receive such considerate treatment while I was met with disregard in a similar situation felt like a dagger to my soul. In that moment, I realized just how far apart we had drifted. I felt a deep sense of betrayal—not just by him, but by the life we had built together.

As these moments accumulated, I felt myself slowly unraveling. The man who once vowed to cherish me now seemed indifferent, his actions speaking louder than the silence that filled our home. I became profoundly sad, and my once vibrant personality began to fade. I withdrew from friends, unable to share the pain of my crumbling marriage, too ashamed to admit that my life was falling apart. I began drinking to help me fall asleep, using wine to drown out the thoughts racing through my mind late at night.

My nights were restless; I would wake in the early hours, staring into the darkness, my mind a whirl of confusion and despair. The loss of sleep took a toll on me. I was perpetually exhausted, and my work—the one thing I had control over—started to suffer. I couldn't focus, and my motivation waned. I felt trapped, caught between the life I had known and the uncertain future that loomed before me. I spent countless nights replaying our life together in my mind, trying to pinpoint the exact moment when everything changed. Was it when I started my business in the seventh year of our marriage? That business became both a blessing and a burden—demanding so much of me while providing the financial stability we needed. I worked 16-hour days, pouring everything I had into making it a success, believing that if I just worked hard enough and became successful enough, everything would be okay.

I made countless sacrifices for our marriage, believing that my dedication could somehow mend the cracks forming between us. I took on the role of the primary breadwinner, paying for almost everything and shouldering the financial burdens without complaint. I was determined not to fail, to keep pushing forward even when everything was falling apart around me. But the more I gave, the more I realized that my efforts were not enough. I was losing myself in the process, my identity swallowed up by the roles I was playing—wife, business owner, caretaker. I was trying to hold everything together, but the weight was becoming unbearable.

I didn't want to admit that I was failing, not just in my marriage but in my attempts to balance everything. I felt a constant tension, a gnawing anxiety that never left me. I became edgy, snapping at small things because I was constantly on edge, feeling like I was on the verge of breaking. There was almost zero joy in my life; every moment was filled with work or tension. I had become resentful, not just towards my husband, but towards the life we had built together—a life that was supposed to be fulfilling but was now draining the very essence of who I was.

The moment of realization was a painful awakening. It was the moment I understood that my marriage was no longer a partnership but a prison. I had to face the harsh truth that I was clinging to a life that no longer existed, holding on to a man who had already let go. The emotional toll was overwhelming, and I knew that something had to change. I could no longer live in denial, pretending that everything was okay when it clearly wasn't. I had to confront the reality of my situation and decide whether to continue down this path of self-destruction or find the courage to break free.

Building the Courage to Leave

The thought of leaving was terrifying. It was not just the fear of ending a marriage but the paralyzing dread of stepping into an unknown future. I spent months wrestling with this decision, trying to gather the courage to leave not just physically but mentally. The man I had shared my life with for two decades had become a stranger. We were living in the same house but in separate worlds, our once-shared dreams now shattered fragments of what used to be.

I began sleeping in a different bedroom, not out of spite but as a painful rehearsal for the life I knew was coming—a life without him. I called it "the weaning," a slow and agonizing process of learning to live without the warmth of his body next to mine. Each night, as I lay alone in that cold, unfamiliar bed, I cried. The tears were a release, a flood of pent-up grief and longing for the love we had lost. I felt like I was losing a part of myself—the part that had grown so accustomed to his presence, his touch, his voice. But this was necessary. I had to prepare myself for a future that felt both inevitable and terrifying.

The fears were overwhelming. I felt like a failure, a person who couldn't make her marriage work. I was terrified of being alone, of starting over at an age when most people were settled and secure. But it wasn't just fear that held me back. There were still things I loved about him, even in those final, fractured years. He kept our home tidy, never showed interest in my money, didn't stay out late, and I never had to worry about infidelity. There were moments of simple companionship that made me question whether leaving was the right choice. I had almost convinced myself to stay because, despite everything, this life was all I knew.

Yet, the emptiness in our relationship was undeniable. His silence cut deeper than any harsh word could. It was a silence filled with indifference, with an absence of love that I could no longer ignore.

Every day, I grappled with a profound sense of loss and grief, mourning the life we once dreamed of building together. I missed the idea of what we could have been more than the reality of what we were. I found myself yearning for a real, passionate love where I would be cherished for who I was, not criticized for who I wasn't. I constantly felt judged and inadequate, as if I could never measure up. Over time, this wore me down, leaving me exhausted and weary from feeling so insufficient. I longed for someone who could love me fully and unconditionally, without trying to change me. I craved support— someone who would cheer me on and believe in my potential, not cut me down with biting comments that stung like a bee about how clever I thought I was. I needed a partner who would lift me higher, not leave me feeling like a shadow of myself.

I confided in my mentor, a woman who had walked this path before me, who had navigated the stormy seas of divorce and emerged stronger on the other side. Her words gave me strength and clarity, helping me see that I was not alone in my struggle. I listened to others who had successfully navigated separation and divorce, drawing inspiration from their stories of resilience and renewal.

There were countless small moments that made me realize I needed to leave— the way he looked past me as if I were invisible, the coldness in his eyes, the indifference in his voice. But the most painful realization was that I was lonelier with him than I was by myself. It was a crushing truth, one that weighed heavily on my heart and soul. I knew then that leaving was not just an option but a necessity. I could no longer live in the shadow of a love that had died, clinging to the remnants of a marriage that no longer brought me joy.

The emotional weight of this decision was almost unbearable. To cope, I turned to meditation, seeking solace in the quiet moments of reflection. I read voraciously, immersing myself in stories of others who had faced similar challenges. I prayed for strength and guidance, and slowly, I began to find a sense of peace. It wasn't easy, but I knew it was necessary. I had to confront my fears, my insecurities, and the reality of what my life had become. I had to choose myself, my happiness, and my future over a past that could no longer sustain me.

The Decision to Move On

Eventually, we had "the talk." It was a conversation that had been looming over us for so long, its weight pressing down on every moment we spent together. I had rehearsed what I wanted to say countless times in my head, but when the moment finally came, the words didn't come out as planned. We sat at our dining table, the same table where we had once shared meals, laughter, and dreams. Now, it felt like a stage set for a final act. The room was quiet, not with tension, but with a heavy sense of finality. His eyes were expressionless, staring past me as if he was already looking into a future where I no longer existed.

We spoke honestly, laying everything bare. He talked about his desires, his dreams for a family and children—a dream I knew I could never fulfill without medical assistance. I had begun the process of in vitro fertilization, but my heart wasn't in it anymore. Sitting there, I realized I couldn't bring a child into this loveless marriage. It would be cruel, even wicked, to bring an innocent life into a situation that was already so broken. The weight of this realization crashed down on me like a wave pulling me under, leaving me gasping for air.

The next morning, I moved like a ghost through the house, my body numb with a mixture of dread and resolve. I packed a small carry-on bag, knowing that in life, the things I truly needed could fit into that bag. I had long realized that you don't need a lot of "stuff" to survive. The material things, the trappings of a life we had built together, felt meaningless now. I took only what was necessary, leaving behind the rest as if shedding a skin that no longer fit.

I asked him to drive me to the airport. Our final journey together was filled with a silence that spoke louder than words ever could.

When we arrived, we hugged for what we both knew would be the last time. It wasn't a passionate embrace, but a respectful one, filled with unspoken words and a silent understanding.

Our bodies communicated what our mouths could not—this was the end. We were wishing each other well in a way that was more about self-preservation than affection. As I pulled away, I felt an emptiness where love once resided, replaced now by a hollow acceptance.

As I boarded the flight to Florida, I felt like a failure. Not because of the separation itself, but because I couldn't make it work. I had poured everything into this marriage, and still, it had crumbled. I was numb on the flight, unable to muster the strength to feel anything. My mind was a blank slate, wiped clean by the harsh reality of my new life. I stared out of the window as the plane took off, but I wasn't really seeing anything. There were no tears, no sense of liberation—just a void where my emotions should have been.

Leaving wasn't just about leaving him; it was about leaving behind an entire chapter of my life, a chapter that had defined me for over two decades. As the plane lifted into the sky, there were no doubts, just a profound emptiness that seemed to swallow everything else.

When I arrived in Florida, the first thing I did was decide to refurbish the apartment I would be staying in. I wanted it to be as elegant as possible—a small act of defiance against the mess my life had become. I was determined to make this place my sanctuary, a space where I could rebuild myself over the next few years. As I looked around the empty apartment, I realized that this was it—my new beginning. But instead of feeling hopeful, I felt a deep, bone- chilling loneliness.

The reality of what I had done, what I had left behind, began to settle in. There was no going back, no undoing the choices that had led me here. I was alone, truly alone for the first time in over twenty years, and I had to figure out how to live again. But in that emptiness, there was also a flicker of something else—a tiny spark of hope that maybe, just maybe, I could find myself again.

The Darkness of Despair

During the separation, I sank into a darkness that felt endless. I became profoundly depressed, the weight of it so heavy that it felt like a physical force pressing down on my chest. There were days when getting out of bed seemed like an insurmountable task. I felt like I was drowning in sadness, and there were moments when I literally felt like throwing in the towel.

I remember one of the darkest days vividly. I was driving my Mercedes-Benz down the street, my mind consumed by a swirling storm of thoughts. Out of nowhere, a voice whispered in my head, urging me to crash the car, to end the pain right there. My hands gripped the steering wheel so tightly that my knuckles turned white, and for a terrifying moment, I considered it. I considered ending it all just to escape the unbearable ache in my chest. On another day, I sat at my desk, staring blankly at my computer screen. My concentration was nonexistent; my mind was a fog of despair. I couldn't think, couldn't work. I was trapped in a cycle of hopelessness, wondering if this was all that was left for me.

The days blurred together. I went an entire week without bathing, the simple act of showering feeling like a monumental effort. I would lie in bed, staring at the ceiling, numb and paralyzed by the emptiness that had taken over my life. I felt worthless, a shell of the person I once was. I questioned my purpose, my worth, my future. I wondered if I would ever find someone who could love me for who I truly was, without judgment or criticism. I felt utterly alone, even when surrounded by people.

One day, I heard a voice in my head telling me to walk out of the house, to leave everything behind. Another voice, softer but insistent, told me to stay, warning me that I was in no state to find my way back home. It was as if I was being torn in two, caught between the urge to escape and the fear of the unknown. The internal battle left me exhausted, drained of all energy and willpower. In these moments of despair, I relied heavily on my psychologist. She became my lifeline, the one person who could see through the darkness and offer a glimmer of hope. I remember one session in particular when I felt like I couldn't go on. She asked me to close my eyes and describe what I wanted my life to look like five years from now. At first, I couldn't see anything—just darkness and emptiness. But she gently guided me, encouraging me to imagine a future where I was happy and fulfilled.

She made me do exercises that showed me I was still relevant to the world, that I still had something to offer. Her words were like a lifeline, pulling me back from the edge of despair.

I prayed daily, my conversations with God raw and unfiltered. I begged Him for peace, for relief from the crushing sadness that threatened to consume me. I knew, deep down, that He would come through for me as He always had, but I found myself pleading for it to happen sooner rather than later. I needed a sign, something to hold onto in the darkness.

Then, slowly, things began to shift. I met someone who helped me find happiness in my loneliness, who showed me that I could still find joy even when I felt utterly alone. It was a small glimmer of light in the darkness, but it was enough to give me hope. I realized that I was not as alone as I had thought, that there were still people in this world who cared about me and wanted to see me thrive.

On the days when the sadness felt overwhelming, I operated on autopilot. I would get up, force myself to bathe, eat, work, and sleep, repeating the motions like a robot. It wasn't living, but it was surviving. And slowly, day by day, I began to feel a little stronger, a little more like myself. My faith became my anchor in the storm, reminding me that I was not alone, that I was loved, and that I would find my way back to the light.

Embracing a New Beginning

I knew I needed a plan to survive when I reached the darkest point of my life. The despair was so overwhelming at times that ending it all seemed like the only escape. I couldn't see a way out of the pain; it consumed every part of me. All I could think about was my marriage and how I had failed. I felt like a joke, a loser, the punchline of some cruel cosmic game. People had predicted that my marriage would fail, and despite doing everything possible to prove them wrong, twenty years later, they were right. The shame was unbearable, and I felt like I had lost everything.

But I knew I had to do something, anything, to keep myself from spiraling further. I needed to find a way to channel the pain, to turn it into something that could sustain me. I threw myself into my business with a relentless drive, working tirelessly to fill the void that had taken root in my heart. I had to keep moving, keep doing, keep distracting myself from the torment that waited in the silence. But even that wasn't enough. I needed something more, something that could completely absorb my focus and help me heal. That's when I decided to pursue a Master's degree in Rhetoric, Composition, and Digital Media—a subject I had always been passionate about but never had the chance to study.

Enrolling in that program was like stepping into a new world, one where I could redefine myself and my future. I buried myself in assignments and presentations, pouring everything I had into my studies. The work was grueling, but it was a lifeline, pulling me out of the darkness one paper, one project at a time. I took on unique assignments, like creating a comic book, something that felt so outside of who I had been, yet strangely fitting for who I was becoming. Learning new things— like virtual reality, augmented reality, and the history of English—felt like a breath of fresh air in a room that had been stifling me for years.

Each day was a battle against the shadows that threatened to swallow me whole. I would wake up, lace up my running shoes, and head to the beach. The long walks and runs along the shore became my sanctuary. The rhythmic pounding of my feet against the sand, the sound of the waves crashing beside me—it was all a release, a way to escape the pain. It was as if, with every step, I was outrunning the ghosts of my past. I met other runners there, people who were also going through their own struggles, and in their company, I found a strange kind of solace. For those brief moments, I wasn't alone in my suffering. Running was my catharsis, my way of cleansing the hurt that had seeped into every corner of my soul.

At first, I clung to the hope of reconciliation. It was what I knew, what felt familiar. I feared starting over, feared the unknown.

And there was another, deeper fear that haunted me—my past. I had been raped at age six, and that trauma had left scars that never fully healed. I had found comfort in the familiarity of my husband's presence; the thought of starting a new sexual relationship with another man was unthinkable. I couldn't imagine sharing that intimacy with anyone else, nor did I want to.

But slowly, painfully, I realized that holding onto something that was already broken wasn't going to fix anything. I wasn't going to achieve my dreams or find happiness in a place where love no longer existed.

Distracting myself from the torment that waited in the silence. But even that wasn't enough. I needed something more, something that could completely absorb my focus and help me heal. That's when I decided to pursue a Master's degree in Rhetoric, Composition, and Digital Media—a subject I had always been passionate about but never had the chance to study.

Enrolling in that program was like stepping into a new world, one where I could redefine myself and my future. I buried myself in assignments and presentations, pouring everything I had into my studies. The work was grueling, but it was a lifeline, pulling me out of the darkness one paper, one project at a time. I took on unique assignments, like creating a comic book, something that felt so outside of who I had been, yet strangely fitting for who I was becoming. Learning new things— like virtual reality, augmented reality, and the history of English—felt like a breath of fresh air in a room that had been stifling me for years.

The turning point came one day when a friend, blunt and brutally honest, told me that my husband didn't even like me. Not love— like. The weight of that word hit me like a ton of bricks. It wasn't about love anymore; it was about the basic decency of liking the person you were with. And if he didn't even like me, what was left? I knew then that I had to move on, that I deserved more than what I was settling for. I deserved to like myself, to love myself enough to let go.

Embracing this new chapter was terrifying. It was like standing at the edge of a cliff, looking down into the abyss, and deciding to jump anyway. I felt empowered by the choice, scared out of my mind, and strangely hopeful all at once. I had no idea what the future held, but I knew I had to take it one day at a time. I leaned on my faith, praying to God for strength and guidance. I spoke to my psychologist, to my mentor, to anyone who would listen. I started writing, pouring my heart onto the page as a way to make sense of the chaos in my mind.

In moments of doubt and exhaustion, when everything seemed overwhelming, I reminded myself why I was doing this. I was doing it for me, for the person I wanted to become, for the life I wanted to live. I told myself that I was stronger than my pain, that I had survived worse and would survive this too. And slowly, day by day, I began to believe it.

Distracting myself from the torment that waited in the silence. But even that wasn't enough. I needed something more, something that could completely absorb my focus and help me heal. That's when I decided to pursue a Master's degree in Rhetoric, Composition, and Digital Media—a subject I had always been passionate about but never had the chance to study.

Embracing Resilience Through Writing

The first time I realized that writing could be a way to process my pain was when I started working on my trilogy, *Limitless*. Initially, it was just a desperate attempt to escape the overwhelming darkness that enveloped me after my separation. I was trying to find a way out of the suffocating sadness, searching for something— anything—that could help me breathe again. But as I wrote, I found myself lost in my thoughts, traveling back to the beginning of my life.

I began to reflect on my journey—how I was born into a hard life, surrounded by challenges that seemed insurmountable at the time. Through writing, I started to unpack the stories of the people who had shaped me, those who had made me recognize that I was truly limitless. These were the individuals who saw something in me when I couldn't see it in myself, who pushed me to believe there was more to life than the pain and hardship I had known. As I wrote about them, I found myself revisiting those moments, feeling the emotions all over again—the fear, the doubt, but also the strength and determination that had carried me through.

The deeper I delved into my writing, the more I saw the power of my own story. I realized that every hardship, every moment of despair, had built me into the person I am today. Writing *Limitless* became a way for me to recognize how far I had come— from a girl who doubted her worth to a woman who had achieved things beyond her wildest dreams. It showed me that I was not defined by my pain but by my ability to rise above it. In those moments of reflection, I discovered my own strength. Writing became a mirror, reflecting back not just my struggles but also my triumphs. It helped me see that I was powerful, that I had always been powerful. And it was through this process that I realized the pain I felt wasn't a weight to drag me down but a source of incredible power that could propel me forward. By writing, I wasn't just processing my pain—I was transforming it into something beautiful, something that could inspire others to recognize their own limitless potential.

But there were also times when the weight of depression felt too much to bear. I remember one day vividly, a day that still haunts me. I was in the depths of despair, feeling utterly lost and alone. In a moment of vulnerability, I reached out to my husband, desperate for some connection, some shred of comfort in the midst of my pain. I laid bare the depths of my suffering, hoping that maybe, just maybe, he could offer me a lifeline. But instead of the compassion I was seeking, I was reminded of the very reason for my pain. It became clear that turning to him was pointless. The realization was crushing but necessary. I had to find solace within myself, in my writing, and in the new beginnings I was forging on my own.

This journey through writing was not just about recounting my past but about forging a new path forward. It was about taking the raw, painful experiences and crafting them into something that could heal and inspire. Writing *Limitless* became my sanctuary, a place where I could embrace my resilience and share it with others who might need it. And through this process, I discovered that even in the darkest of times, there is always a flicker of hope waiting to be uncovered.

A Shift in the Darkness

The words on the phone cut through me like a knife. In that moment, I felt the ground beneath me crumble. Shame washed over me in waves, pulling me under, drowning me in self-doubt and regret. I felt so exposed, so utterly foolish for seeking solace from the person who had become the source of my torment. I wanted to disappear, to hide away from the world and from myself. I felt broken, like all the pieces of me had shattered, and I couldn't see a way to put them back together.

I sank deeper into depression. The weight of his words pressed down on me, suffocating me, filling every corner of my mind with darkness. I felt like I had lost everything—my husband, my marriage, my sense of self. I questioned everything: my worth, my choices, my future. I was embarrassed, ashamed that I had let myself be so vulnerable, so desperate. I wanted to hide, to retreat into the shadows where no one could see the depth of my pain, where I could pretend that none of this was happening.

But then, something shifted. In the midst of my despair, I heard a small voice inside me—a whisper, a spark of defiance. It told me that I couldn't let this be the end of my story. I had been through too much, fought too hard, to let this break me. I realized that if I continued to hide, if I let the shame and the pain consume me, then I was letting him win. I was letting the darkness win.

I thought about all the times I had faced challenges before, all the times I had been knocked down but found a way to get back up. I remembered the strength that had carried me through so many battles, the resilience that had kept me going when I thought I couldn't take another step. I realized that I still had that strength within me, that I still had the power to choose how my story would continue.

Rising from the Ashes

It was then that I made a decision—to stop letting my past define me, to stop allowing someone else's words to dictate my worth. It was time to rebuild, to take the broken pieces of myself and forge something new. It wasn't easy. Each step forward felt like wading through thick mud, but I kept going. I told myself that every small victory— getting out of bed, completing a task, allowing myself to smile—was proof that I was healing.

I leaned even more into my writing. The more I wrote, the more I realized that this was my path to freedom. I wasn't just writing to process the pain; I was writing to reclaim my narrative. I wrote about survival, about the grit it takes to pull yourself out of despair, about the hope that exists even in the darkest moments. My words became my lifeline, each sentence a testament to my resilience. It was a way to rebuild the identity I thought I had lost. Through writing, I began to feel empowered again.

I reached out to my support system—my psychologist, my closest friends, and my family. Slowly, I started to rebuild relationships that were rooted in love and care, not in fear and dependence. These connections reminded me of who I was at my core, someone who was not defined by a failed marriage but by the strength to endure and to thrive.

It wasn't a linear journey. There were days when the darkness would creep back in, when I would doubt my progress and feel the weight of loneliness. But I held on to the spark that had ignited within me, refusing to let it be extinguished. I learned to find beauty in small moments, to celebrate the fact that I was still standing, still fighting.

And so, little by little, I rose from the ashes of my past. I began to craft a new vision for my future, one that wasn't tied to anyone else's expectations or judgments. I let go of the shame that had bound me for so long, allowing myself to embrace my own strength and worth.

I realized that the ending I had feared wasn't really an ending at all—it was the beginning of something new, something more beautiful than I could have ever imagined. My pain had not been in vain. It had shaped me, strengthened me, and led me to a deeper understanding of who I was. I wasn't just surviving anymore—I was thriving, reclaiming my life on my own terms.

The Healing Power of Word

So, I got up. I refused to let myself be swallowed by the darkness. I chose to fight, to keep moving forward, even when every part of me wanted to curl up and disappear. I prayed for strength, for the courage to face another day. I reminded myself that with God, all things are possible, even when it feels like the world is falling apart. I chose to believe that this pain, as unbearable as it was, could be transformed into something meaningful, something powerful. I chose to believe that I was stronger than my circumstances, stronger than my pain.

And with that belief, I found the will to continue. I put one foot in front of the other, day after day, even when it felt impossible. I chose to rise, to rebuild, to find a new way forward. And slowly, I began to see that the darkness wasn't the end of my story—it was just the beginning of a new chapter.

As I continued writing and working, doubt and fear were constant companions. I questioned every word, every page, every decision. I poured my heart and soul into my trilogy, Limitless, but the more I wrote, the more I doubted myself. I remember thinking, This is terrible. Who am I kidding? I convinced myself that no one would want to read it, that it was a pointless endeavor. The fear of failure hung over me like a dark cloud, whispering in my ear, telling me I wasn't good enough, that my story didn't matter.

I was ready to give up. I wanted to throw the manuscript in the trash and pretend it never existed. But in a moment of vulnerability, I decided to share my work with my friend, Dr. Derry. I was terrified of what he might say, bracing myself for criticism and confirmation of all my worst fears. When he finished reading, I waited for the words that would seal my fate.

Instead, he looked at me with a kind smile and said, "Shalette, the book is not perfect. But frankly, no book is. That's why people have second editions." His words were like a lifeline, pulling me out of the sea of doubt that threatened to drown me. In that moment, he gave me the gift of perspective. He made me realize that perfection wasn't the goal—progress was. He reminded me that every writer has moments of uncertainty, that every book has flaws, and that's okay.

Tears filled my eyes as his words sank in. I felt a deep sense of gratitude for his honesty, his encouragement, and his belief in me when I couldn't believe in myself. He didn't just give me feedback; he gave me confidence. He gave me permission to be imperfect, to take a risk, to put my work out into the world despite my fears. He made me see that the value of my story wasn't in its perfection but in its authenticity, in the courage it took to write it.

Thank you, Dr. Derry, for seeing what I couldn't see. For lifting me up when I was ready to fall. For being the voice of reason in my chaos, the steady hand that guided me back to my path. You helped me find the strength to continue, to push through the fear and doubt, to believe in myself and my story. Without you, Limitless might never have seen the light of day. You reminded me that it's not about being perfect—it's about being brave enough to share your truth. And for that, I will always be grateful.

A Daily Commitment to Healing

During those difficult times, my writing process was both my salvation and my struggle. I made a commitment to myself that no matter how sad or depressed I felt, I would write four pages each day. It didn't matter if those pages were filled with pain, uncertainty, or even anger. I just knew I had to keep going. Some days, the words flowed easily, like a release of everything bottled up inside me. But most days, it was a battle—a battle against the weight of my own despair, a battle against the voice in my head that told me to give up.

There were times when I would sit at my desk, my hands trembling, staring at a blank page with tears streaming down my face. The sadness was overwhelming, pressing down on me so hard that I could barely breathe. But I kept writing.

I wrote through the sadness, the doubt, and the fear. I wrote through the memories of my failed marriage and the crushing loneliness that followed. I wrote about my hopes for the future, even when they seemed distant and unreachable. Writing was my lifeline, my way of processing everything I had gone through, everything I was still going through. It was the one thing that made sense when nothing else did.

In those moments, I realized that writing wasn't just a way to escape my pain—it was a way to confront it, to make sense of it, to transform it. Every word I wrote was a step toward healing, a step toward reclaiming my story, my strength, and my life. It was through writing that I began to see that I wasn't defined by my past or my pain—I was defined by my resilience, by my ability to keep going, to keep fighting, to keep believing in the possibility of something better.

Writing Through the Storm

I wrote through the tears, the frustration, and the heartache. My tears would fall onto the paper, smudging the ink, but I refused to let them stop me. I wrote because it was the only thing that kept me from falling apart, the only thing that made sense when everything else felt like chaos.

I got lost in my thoughts, in the stories I was creating. Writing became a way for me to escape my reality, to pour out all the pain and confusion onto the page. Each word, each sentence was like a step forward in the dark, a step toward something I couldn't yet see but hoped was there. I clung to my routine like a lifeline. Even when I felt like I had nothing left to give, I would sit down and write those four pages. It was a promise I made to myself—a promise to keep going, no matter what.

Some of those pages were filled with raw, unfiltered emotion. They were messy and imperfect, but they were real. They were pieces of my soul laid bare, moments of truth captured in words. And as hard as it was, as painful as it sometimes felt, I knew I had to persevere. Because with each page I wrote, I was reclaiming a part of myself. I was finding my strength, my resilience, and my will to keep fighting.

Writing became my way of pushing through the darkness, of reminding myself that I was still here, still fighting. It wasn't easy. There were days when I wanted to quit, when the pain was too much and the doubt was too strong. But I didn't. I kept going, page after page, tear after tear, finding my way through the storm one word at a time. And in those words, I found myself again.

Recognition and Faith

Seeing my work recognized and appreciated, especially the "Ability Test Workbook," was incredibly validating. Knowing that thousands of children were using my books, that my work was making a difference in their education, was a profound realization.

It was a reminder that all the hard work, all the sacrifices, had not been in vain. It was a testament to my resilience, to my determination to turn my pain into something meaningful and impactful.

My faith also played a crucial role in helping me through particularly dark moments. I leaned on my belief that "With God, all things are possible." I prayed for strength, for guidance, for the courage to keep going when everything felt like it was falling apart. My faith became a source of hope, a reminder that I was not alone, that there was a higher purpose to my struggles.

The Journey and Sacrifices

Th journey wasn't without its sacrifices. There were many times when it was hard to keep up with the demands of writing and studying. I had countless assignments, papers to write, group work to complete. It was exhausting, both emotionally and physically. I had to force myself to rest numerous times, even developing a habit of taking over-the- counter sleeping pills to help me sleep.

But through it all, I never felt like giving up on writing. My first academic book was a real success, and that gave me the motivation to keep going. Looking back, the hardest part was believing in myself, believing that what I was writing was good enough, that it was worthy. It took a lot of inner work, a lot of reflection, and a lot of support from the people around me to truly believe in my own strength and resilience.

Transformation Through Writing

Writing was my way of transforming my pain into something meaningful, something that could inspire others. It was a journey of self-discovery, of healing, and ultimately, of empowerment. And I wouldn't trade it for anything in the world.

The truth is, we all face moments of doubt, pain, and fear. But it's in those moments that we discover our strength, our resilience, and our capacity to rise above. Writing taught me that even in my darkest moments, I had the power to create something beautiful, something lasting. It was my way of taking control of my story, of turning my pain into something that could make a difference. And in doing so, I found my purpose, my voice, and my strength.

Thriving Beyond Measure

After the divorce, I soared. Yes, I soared. I already had a PhD, an EdS, an MBA, and a BSc, but it was my new degree in rhetoric that truly set me free. It unlocked a passion for writing that I never knew existed. I just started writing and writing. Each word was a step forward, each sentence a leap away from my past. And as the pages filled, so did my spirit. I found a voice I didn't know I had, a power that had been lying dormant, waiting for this very moment to emerge.

I also began speaking more frequently, presenting at education conferences on topics like technology in education and brain training. Eventually, I expanded to women's conferences, sharing insights on how to succeed independently. I traveled to over 20 countries and across four continents. From bustling cities to serene landscapes, I stood before audiences and shared my journey, my pain, my triumphs. One thing that traveling allowed me to see is that life goes on without you every day. The world is moving, things are happening, and I realized I had two choices: be left behind or jump right in and make my mark.

My travels, particularly to Japan, were transformative. Speaking at the Asian Conference on Education was a highlight. There, I spoke on the impact of technology on memory—an area few had ventured into. People gravitated toward me and my message, eager to learn and engage. The requests for speaking engagements began pouring in, and I saw clearly for the first time that I had so much to offer the world. I realized I have a purpose to live, a message to share. It wasn't just about surviving the divorce anymore; it was about thriving, about soaring higher than I ever imagined.

To thrive after divorce, I sought professional help. My therapist was incredible; she pulled me out of the depths of self-pity and depression. I started focusing on my physical fitness, hiring a personal trainer and joining a gym to build strength both inside and out. I delved deep into introspection and meditation, reconnecting with myself and with God. I even wrote a book titled *God Is Still in the Miracle Working Business*, which became another avenue of healing and inspiration for me and others.

I stayed busy, set goals, and worked relentlessly toward them. I bought my dream house, a sanctuary that became a symbol of my independence. I made sure my mom lived well, ensuring she never had to worry about anything again. I built a retirement plan that allows me to live comfortably and securely. These goals weren't just dreams—they were my roadmap to a new life.

I also ventured into real estate, which I believe is the true path to wealth. I noticed that every successful person I admired had some form of real estate in their portfolio. So, I bought several properties and expanded my Airbnb business, turning it into a successful venture. I loved decorating those spaces, making them beautiful havens for my guests. It wasn't just about making money; it was about creating experiences, both for myself and for others.

Looking back, I see how far I have come. The woman who once feared life without her husband has become a thriving business owner, a successful author, and a confident speaker. I was going to achieve the goals I set out to achieve when I was a teenager. I realized that I could do it solo. I changed my looks, shaved my head, started wearing dots on my forehead, and embraced my new identity with pride and confidence. I connected more with my inner self, found strength in my struggles, purpose in my pain, and success beyond my wildest dreams.

For anyone going through a similar experience, know this: Never give up. Seek professional help. Surround yourself with positivity and set goals that will take your mind off your problems. Find something that ignites your passion. Thriving means getting fit mentally, financially, emotionally, physically, and spiritually. It's about finding balance in every area of your life and not letting any one aspect dominate you.

My journey wasn't easy, but it was worth it. I am living proof that you can turn your pain into purpose. The success of my books—selling hundreds of thousands of copies each—propelled me to continue writing and speaking. The expansion of my Airbnb business gave me a new sense of independence and accomplishment. My travels opened my eyes to the world and showed me that there is so much more out there than our limited perspectives.

Today, thriving means embracing every moment, every challenge, every opportunity with open arms and an open heart. It means constantly evolving, continually growing, and always pushing beyond what I thought possible. And I know, without a doubt, that if I can do it, so can you. Embrace your journey, for it is uniquely yours. Find your strength, discover your purpose, and soar higher than you ever imagined possible.

SECTION FOUR

THRIVING IN
WIDOWHOOD

MAKING A CONSCIOUS EFFORT AS A WIDOW SURVIVING GRIEF

BARRIE THOMAS

Grief is defined as the profound anguish experienced after a significant loss. The process of coping with this heartache often takes you through several stages before you can regain any semblance of normalcy. While time does, in many ways, help heal wounds, the amount of time required to traverse these stages of sorrow depends greatly on the individual's inner strength, emotional resilience, and ability to process the grief.

Courage, resilience, and fortitude are often synonymous with strength, but each of these qualities plays a crucial role in helping you navigate life after an overwhelming loss.

Moving forward is never easy—especially when what you've lost was a vital part of your existence.

I've learned that grief is often categorized into five stages: Denial, Anger, Bargaining, Depression, and Acceptance. I wouldn't reference these stages if I hadn't lived through them myself. For context, I met and married a wonderful man, and together, we raised three beautiful children. My life was full and rich with joy. But in 2019, during the category six hurricane that devastated the Bahamas, I lost my entire immediate family to the waters. The irony is not lost on me: these very waters, which had provided for us for years, claimed the lives of my husband and my three children. The sea had always been a source of sustenance and serenity for us, as my husband's livelihood was connected to it, and our children shared his deep love for the ocean. But during that storm, what had once blessed us with life turned into a force of devastation, snatching away everything I held dear. Seventy-four people were reported dead in that storm, and more than two hundred and forty-five are still missing. My family was among them.

Denial

Denial is the mind's way of protecting you from a reality too painful to bear. In those early days after the hurricane, I lived in a state of disbelief. I couldn't reconcile the enormity of my loss with the life I had known just days before. It felt as if I had been thrust into an alternate reality—one that I could neither understand nor accept. I clung to the hope that somehow, I'd wake up and find that none of it had happened. But denial, though it shields you momentarily, prevents you from confronting the harsh truth. It delays the inevitable reckoning with reality.

Anger

As denial began to wane, anger took its place. I found myself growing less tolerant of things that had once been easy to overlook. The smallest irritations would send me spiraling into rage, and I wanted to lash out at the world. How could life continue around me as if nothing had happened? How could people smile, laugh, and carry on while my life had been shattered? I was angry at everything and everyone—at God, at fate, even at myself. I wanted to scream, to demand answers, to make sense of the senseless. Anger, in its own way, gave me energy, something to feel besides the overwhelming sadness. But it also kept me isolated, stuck in a loop of resentment.

Bargaining

Bargaining came in the form of desperate conversations with God. I wanted so badly to undo what had happened, to find a way to bring my family back. I prayed endlessly, negotiating with God. "Lord, if you bring my family back to me, I will do anything. I will live a life of service, I will give up everything else I love—just please, let them return." I begged and bargained, trying to strike deals that would never be. But nothing changed.

My family did not come back. Bargaining was a futile attempt to gain control in a situation where control had been stripped from me. It was the mind's way of seeking solace, but ultimately, it only deepened the sorrow when no answers came.

Depression

As the reality of my loss settled in, depression enveloped me. The weight of my grief became too much to bear. Everything I had known and loved was gone, and I couldn't find my way back to the light. I turned to alcohol in an attempt to numb the pain, hoping that the temporary escape would ease the unbearable emptiness inside me. But inebriation was only a fleeting respite. The reality always crashed back in, heavier and harder to face than before. My depression was all-consuming, leaving me feeling hollow, disconnected, and adrift in a sea of despair. I didn't just miss my family—I missed the person I had been before the storm, the woman who had been whole, happy, and unbroken.

Acceptance

Acceptance did not come easily, nor did it arrive all at once. It crept in slowly, like the first rays of sunlight after a long, dark night. It didn't mean that the pain was gone or that I no longer grieved for my family, but it did mean that I began to understand that my life, though irreparably changed, still had value and purpose. I remembered the person my husband had always believed me to be—a strong, resilient woman capable of surviving even the most unimaginable pain. Gradually, I began to reclaim that identity. I knew I could not live in the past, so I chose to press forward. Acceptance wasn't a one-time event; it was a continuous process of choosing to live, to rebuild, and to move beyond the wreckage of my loss.

My experience reminds me of a quote by Dr. Mansha Khemlani: "Grief is like waves. When it surges, you fear being swept away. In time, you will learn to surf those waves and also enjoy the tranquility that calmer waters bring… until the next big wave." This analogy resonated deeply with me. The waves of grief never fully stop, but with time, I have learned to ride them, to find peace even in the midst of the storm.

Here are three points to take away:

Embrace the Grieving Process Fully

It's important to recognize and accept each stage of grief—Denial, Anger, Bargaining, Depression, and Acceptance. Don't rush through these stages or suppress your emotions. Let yourself feel the pain, the sadness, and the anger, knowing that it is all part of healing. Grief isn't something you can "get over," but rather something you learn to live with as you grow stronger.

Seek Professional Help and Lean on Support

Whether through therapy, counseling, or simply talking to someone who understands, seeking professional support is crucial. Surround yourself with positive influences and don't hesitate to ask for help when you need it. Isolation can deepen the pain, but sharing your burden can provide relief and perspective.

Find Purpose in Pain

Channel your grief into something meaningful—whether that's writing, creating, or pursuing a passion that gives you purpose. Use your pain as a catalyst for growth, and let it drive you toward new goals. By focusing on something that fulfills you, you can transform your loss into a source of resilience and strength. It may never leave you but you can give it purpose.

UNDERSTANDING THE 'WHY' OF WIDOWHOOD

DR. JOAN WRIGHT-GOOD

Exodus 22:22-24

"Do not take advantage of the widow or the fatherless. If you do and they cry out to me, I will certainly hear their cry. My anger will be aroused, and I will kill you with the sword; your wives will become widows and your children fatherless."

Strong words, aren't they? Truth is there are over 498 scriptures about widows in the bible, God is indeed concerned about widows and orphans. In fact, He said in Psalm 68:5, God is a "defender of widows in His holy habitation." In other words, even from heaven, the holiest place in the universe, God looks down and takes pride in widows that are in Him. Defending them is a priority to His.

Hi, my name is Joan, and if you're just hearing about me or have just met me, you probably already know that I fit into every category mentioned in this book, but most recently, as a widow. I have been a mother— a teen mother at that— and a single mother for years. I became a wife at the age of 25 and divorced at 33, experiencing life as a divorcée in full force. I found love again and remarried, but 13 years later, I became a widow. My assignment in this project is to speak to widows.

I wrote a book in 2023 about my experience as a widow, but I made sure it was filled with educational information for girlfriends, fiancées, wives, and widows—sort of like preparation before, during, and what happens if they become widows. I will take some elements of that book to add to what I will share here, but if you haven't picked up a copy of my book, ***The Miseducation of Widowhood: 10 Things Every Wife Should Know About Managing, Coping & Dealing with the Journey***, do yourself a favor, stop reading now, and scan this code with your phone to order it!

Thank me later!

Widowhood: The New Normal

Widowhood is a journey no one ever anticipates, yet it arrives unannounced, reshaping every facet of life. In the quiet aftermath of loss, the roles you once embodied—wife, CEO, mother, and woman of faith—shift dramatically. The weight of grief becomes a constant companion, but so too is the call to keep moving forward. How does one navigate a life forever altered while still fulfilling the responsibilities of leadership, faith, and personal well-being? This was the question I had to confront every day.

In the months after my husband's passing, I found myself grappling with an entirely new reality. I had become an empty nester, as my youngest child moved out to attend college. My life was filled with decisions that tested my strength, patience, and faith. Some days, the struggle lay in running my business with clarity and focus—because business, after all, does not care about trauma. On other days, it was simply the act of getting out of bed that felt monumental. Balancing grief with the demands of lawsuits brought on by my husband's sudden death, alongside business, ministry, and personal healing, became not just a challenge but a daily act of survival. There were moments I found myself grappling with feelings of betrayal, disappointment, and anger—feelings I had to work hard to forgive. How could he leave me like this? This is the story of how I transitioned from merely surviving to truly thriving—a journey fueled by faith, resilience, and a renewed vision for life. I share it with you so that you, too, may find strength and hope in your journey.

When most Christians pray for marriage, they imagine a wonderful experience with their dream person and a fairytale wedding. They believe that when they pray, the person who ticks most of their boxes must be the answer to their prayers. Yet, the real truth about marriage is that the wedding is simply an event—marriage itself is a ministry. Some people thrive in this ministry, while others struggle. Our marriage was life-changing—filled with new experiences, costly mistakes, and profound lessons. It was a mixture of salt and sugar, bitter and sweet, water and fire. Marriage is perhaps the most expensive institution to attend, and while some make it to the end and walk the stage at graduation, others take gap semesters to catch up on the curriculum. We were that couple who took those gap semesters, but we always returned with massive lessons, experiences that could only have been shaped by our time together. I always say that I graduated from "Deane Harold Good University"—the lessons from this experience are deeply embedded in who I am today.

By 2021, the ugly disease my husband had struggled with resurfaced once again. For years, we had been on a roller coaster, seeking healing and trying to get past this recurring condition. It was a condition that popped up repeatedly—sometimes four, five times a year or more. It made it difficult for me to juggle my roles as a business owner, minister, mother, and wife. I was exhausted, so when we learned that we would face this challenge yet again, I wasn't exactly optimistic. The rest of the year was filled with discussions about what was best for our family. We had already suffered so much trying to 'fix' things. Every time we thought we had achieved healing, we would find ourselves back at square one. On December 31, 2021, my husband experienced his final struggle with this illness. After a sudden cardiac arrest, he spent two days in a coma before passing away.

Grieving the death of a spouse is devastating—especially when it happens unexpectedly or when your relationship was not in the best place. It's every couple's dream to spend eternity together. No one gets married planning for an early ending. So when death comes—whether you are happily married, separated, or divorced—it leaves a profound heartache. The overwhelming sense of loss is often accompanied by guilt, grief, and even physical pain. Some may feel numb or shocked. For me, grief was the first stage of widowhood, a period when I had to come to terms with the fact that a part of me was gone forever. No matter how many scriptures are quoted about seeing them again in heaven, the reality is that you will never see them again in the flesh. The shock of this can take a long time to process, and everyone's timeline for healing is different.

Navigating this new normal is hard for anyone, but it can be even more difficult without financial security or preparation. So, my first piece of advice for a widow reading this chapter is this:

1. Communication is Key

Have ongoing financial discussions with your spouse—not just once, but quarterly, bi-yearly, and annually. Never assume that the decisions made about insurance or savings during dating, on your wedding day, or even in the good years, will remain the same.

Review your financial details together. How much money do you jointly have? What happens to personal accounts in the event of a tragedy? Does anyone else have power of attorney? Who are the beneficiaries of life insurance policies? Make a vow that no matter what issues arise in your relationship, nothing will change regarding how you or your children will be taken care of. Insist on being informed of any changes to your financial arrangements, and consult with a family lawyer or estate planning attorney about your assets. Surprises in this area can be overwhelming after the loss of a spouse.

2. Embrace Grace Over Perfection

Give yourself permission to grieve and heal at your own pace. The expectations of being a leader or caregiver do not vanish, but they must be balanced with grace. It's okay to not have everything together all the time. Prioritize self-compassion over perfection. Allow yourself space to feel, process, and move forward without guilt.

Healing is not linear, and that's okay.

3. Delegate and Build a Strong Support System

You don't have to carry every burden alone. Whether in business or your personal life, seek help when needed. Surround yourself with a trusted team at work who can step in when necessary. Lean on your community—family, friends, church—for emotional and practical support. Delegating isn't a sign of weakness; it's an act of wisdom and self-care.

Lastly, consider setting up a trust account to secure your financial future and provide stability for both your business and personal life. This legal tool ensures that your assets are managed and distributed according to your wishes, giving you peace of mind and protecting your loved ones from unnecessary financial burdens.

Remember, there is no timeline for healing on the journey of widowhood. You'll know when you are ready. What you don't heal today can manifest as pain tomorrow, so give yourself the space to heal before you move on.

4. Prioritize Self-Care and Mental Health

Grieving takes an immense toll on both emotional and physical health. It's important to prioritize self-care and seek professional help if needed. Regular check-ins with a therapist, support group, or pastoral counselor can provide guidance through the emotional ups and downs of widowhood. Mindfulness practices, meditation, or journaling can also help in processing complex emotions.

5. *Give Yourself Permission to Redefine Your Identity*

After the death of a spouse, many widows feel a profound sense of lost identity. Roles that once defined you, such as "wife," may no longer feel applicable, and this shift can feel destabilizing. Take time to rediscover who you are as an individual. This might involve reconnecting with passions, hobbies, or career goals that you might have sidelined. Redefining your identity beyond your marriage can help you find new purpose and fulfillment in life.

6. *Don't Rush Into Major Life Changes*

After a significant loss, it can be tempting to make major life changes in an effort to cope or move forward. However, it's often best to take time before making any major decisions, such as selling a home, moving to a new city, or changing careers. Grief can cloud judgment, and waiting until you feel more emotionally stable will help ensure that decisions are made with a clear mind.

7. *Embrace New Beginnings While Honoring the Past*

It's important to find a balance between cherishing the memories of your spouse and embracing new possibilities in life. Creating new traditions, finding joy in different activities, and opening yourself to new relationships or experiences does not diminish your love for your spouse. Allow yourself to live fully while still holding onto the parts of your past that are meaningful.

8. Stay Connected to a Larger Community

Widowhood can be an isolating experience. Staying connected to a community— whether it's through church, volunteer work, or a social group—can help you combat loneliness and provide a sense of belonging. Being part of a larger community not only offers emotional support but can also help you feel grounded and connected to a bigger purpose beyond your personal loss.

However, all the advice above is incomplete without considering Paul's counsel on death, as outlined in 1 Thessalonians 4:13-14. Paul writes, *"But I do not want you to be ignorant, brethren, concerning those who have fallen asleep (died), lest you sorrow (grieve/mourn) as others who have no hope. For if we believe that Jesus died and rose again, even so God will bring with Him those who sleep (have died) in Jesus (as believers)."* In other words, do not let widowhood define you. You have an eternal hope, and thus, your response to death, grief, and mourning should reflect the assurance of that hope, rather than the despair of those without it.

But the biggest lessons of them all is, *What Happened Was Never a Mistake: There is a Biblical (Big) Picture.*

In John 11:3-4, 35-43, we read about a moment that deeply speaks to the mystery of God's will and how we must learn to surrender to His greater purpose:

"So the sisters sent a message to him: 'Lord, the one YOU LOVE is sick.' When Jesus heard it, he said, 'This sickness will not end in death but is for the glory of God, so that the Son of God may be glorified through it.' When he heard that Lazarus was sick, he stayed two more days in the place where he was."

Later, when Jesus arrived, some of the Jews said, "See how he loved him!" But others criticized, saying, "He opened the blind man's eyes but could not stop this man from dying?"

But Jesus knew something they didn't. He raised his eyes and prayed:

"Father, I thank you that you heard me. I know that you always hear me, but I said this because of the crowd standing here, so that they may believe you sent me." After this, Jesus called out, "Lazarus, come out!" And Lazarus came forth.

The people around Jesus expected Him to heal Lazarus when he was sick, but Jesus intentionally allowed him to die, knowing that a greater miracle was about to take place. Many criticized Jesus for not intervening sooner, but they missed the bigger picture. Their self-centered, limited perspective blinded them to the miraculous work of God that was about to unfold. They thought it was about a personal outcome but God is always concerned about a universal outcome. Sometimes, we too have a self-imposed, narcissistic, narrow view of faith—thinking that it's all about us and our immediate relief, our blessing and our testimony. But what we must remember is that it's not always about us.

Sometimes, the suffering we endure is not just for our growth or for our story—it's for the unbelievers around us to witness the glory of God. We won't always understand why God allows certain things to happen. That's why we must pray for His will, not ours. If God allows you to suffer publicly for His sake, He will raise you up publicly for His glory—not in your time, but in His.

God could have prevented the passing of your spouse, but we cannot insert ourselves into His plans. Instead, we must adjust to His will. When we shift our perspective and surrender our understanding to God's greater purpose, the healing process becomes smoother. We begin to see that even in our most painful moments, God is weaving a story of redemption, hope, and ultimately, His glory.

A PHOENIX RISING FROM THE ASHES

LULU ORANGE TYSON

As the daughter of Haitian immigrant parents, I have faced my share of challenges. Although I was born in the United States, I grew up navigating a world through my parents' eyes. My experiences as a child were shaped by moments that have defined who I am today, one of which was witnessing my parents' occupation. As immigrants, they had limited job options, and often took on roles that were far from desirable.

One such role was as grove pickers. Born in Florida, where the orange is the state fruit and where my parents worked as orange grove pickers, it's a striking coincidence that my birth last name is Orange, from my mother's side. This job, though it provided for us as a family, was grueling. Imagine climbing trees and picking oranges in 100-degree weather— it was a brutal existence. Yet, my parents persevered, always operating in survival mode despite the obstacles they faced.

Reflecting on these experiences now as an adult, I realize that I have always been in "survival mode," learning to adapt to whatever came my way.

I Do

Handsome and charming, Charlie Tyson was everything I had hoped for in a life partner—a man who embraced all aspects of me with love and acceptance. His charisma and infectious smile captured my heart. As the Beyoncé song goes, "He had me at hello." Charlie had a unique way of making me feel special, always offering a compliment about my looks or celebrating my accomplishments.

When he proposed, I was eager to spend my life with him, and without hesitation, I said "I do." The love I saw in his eyes when he gazed at me was profound and genuine. I was overjoyed and began planning an elaborate wedding—something that, while not essential, he willingly indulged in with his input and support. He often reassured me, saying, "Baby, we could live under a bridge as long as I'm with you!"

Our wedding took place on September 1, 2012, surrounded by family and friends. It was a day filled with unforgettable memories and joy—a day I will cherish forever. We danced the night away, and the very next day, we set off for our honeymoon in Honolulu, Hawaii, eager to begin this new chapter of our lives together.

Faith In Fertility

I was blessed to acquire two bonus sons in our marriage, and we also wanted to try to have at least one child together. The journey, however, was not the most conventional, as we were diagnosed with infertility challenges. Little did we know at the time that this would be an extensive journey. Going through this process occasionally tested our marriage, with hormone medications, appointments, and timed intercourse all contributing to unwanted emotional responses. We wanted a baby so badly that we were willing to endure the growing pains associated with having a child. The time invested and the failed treatments sometimes put a huge strain on our relationship.

Then, we received the call: *"Congratulations, you're pregnant."* It was emotional and a sign of relief that we could indeed create a life together.

No Heartbeat

After all the appointments and hearing a viable heartbeat for the first three months, I was ready to transition to an OBGYN who would manage the remainder of the pregnancy. I attended the appointment alone because Charlie had to be at work for a meeting. He had been incredibly faithful and supportive throughout, always committed to being there for me. I didn't mind him missing this appointment as I thought I was receiving my "graduation papers."

As I lay down and awaited the doctor to scan my belly, the atmosphere was unusually quiet. The doctor, normally chatty, was silent. More importantly, I didn't hear the baby's heartbeat and saw the lifeless body of a fetus floating on the monitor. I emitted a loud screech and cry, experiencing a pain so deep I had never felt before. The baby I had envisioned holding in my arms would be no more. The office allowed me to grieve and gave me a moment. They called my husband to deliver the news. We were heartbroken. Our forever angel baby will live in our hearts forever.

Pain To Purpose

As a family, we decided to take some time off to focus on living and healing. I joined a fitness group to concentrate on getting into the best shape of my life. Despite my efforts, I couldn't help but think of our baby. I joined support groups and discovered I was not alone. I wanted to share my story of healing and hope to help others facing similar challenges.

An organization called "Footprints of Angels" reached out to me, inviting me to be their keynote speaker for women who longed to be mothers and had experienced miscarriage or stillbirth. Through my pain, I found purpose. I was able to support other women on their journey to motherhood. I channeled my energy into improving my physical fitness while focusing on my mental health and spirituality. My faith in God and Jesus Christ has always been my foundation. This support was crucial for me to continue thriving and surviving during this time. I not only joined support groups for those with angel babies but also a weekly prayer line to help me and my family with our challenges. This prayer line, led by the late Pastor Clifton Gay III, became a significant part of our lives.

Census Angel

We decided to start trying again but were unsure where to begin. I was working part-time for the Census Bureau. Although I was overqualified, I wanted to gain experience working for the government. I knocked on doors and was often met with reluctance from people unwilling to provide information. One day, I knocked on the door of a very pregnant woman who looked around my age. We began chatting, and she shared her fertility challenges with me. I immediately felt a connection and, with tears, asked her for help. She referred me to a well- known physician specializing in helping women like me conceive. I called that very day and made an appointment to start the journey again. I was so excited that I rushed home to tell my husband. He was cautious and didn't want to get his hopes up, fearing we might face the same hurt as before.

Heart to Heart

After we got married, Charlie began experiencing worsening heart troubles. Despite maintaining a healthy diet and adhering to his medication regimen, his condition deteriorated. He was determined not to let his heart issues interfere with our dream of having a child. The new doctor assured him that his condition would not affect the treatment. This doctor was different; he began our meetings with prayer and expressed his unwavering faith in God. He would often say, "God is doing the work; I am merely a vessel!" I felt a deep sense of comfort with him. We were given the green light to proceed with transferring our baby and were excited about the possibility of becoming parents. However, we were met with disappointing news: the transfer did not work. This happened two more times, leaving me numb to the bad news. The faith-driven doctor suggested stopping all treatments and praying that the transfer would work naturally, without medications. He called it a "Natural IVF" cycle. He prayed with us and reminded us that as believers, God could grant our heart's desires. We had only two viable frozen embryos left and proceeded with the transfer.

Heart Beats

We received the news that not only did we have one viable heartbeat, but two. We graduated past the three-month mark and transitioned to an OBGYN who also specialized in high-risk pregnancies. I was determined to do everything possible to keep my babies healthy so I could meet and hold them. We were thrilled about becoming twin parents. The times were challenging, as the world was grappling with a devastating virus that claimed many lives. I had to be extra cautious. We kept in prayer, and at each appointment, I received updates on the babies' development. Unfortunately, one of the embryos showed an abnormality, and we were faced with another difficult decision as a family. I remember dropping to my knees and asking God for a sign that everything would be okay. He reminded me of the sign in the form of the steady heartbeats still present within me. These were my miracle babies, and nothing would stop us from having them.

Noah and Jonah Arrives

We made it to 38 weeks and 1 day. They entered the world on January 29, 2022, in an unconventional manner. Jonah was delivered vaginally, while Noah arrived via C-section due to his breech position. Hospital staff were amazed to witness both procedures during the same birth. I allowed students to observe the delivery, and it turned into a grand lesson. Jonah and Noah were born; Noah needed to stay in the NICU for three weeks, while Jonah was able to go home.

Our Forever Angel

With our babies finally in our arms, we prepared to celebrate with a Vow Renewal and Baby Dedication event, marking ten years of marriage and the arrival of our miracle twins. It was a once-in-a-lifetime event. However, shortly afterward, the unimaginable happened—Charlie's heart took its last beat just before the twins' first birthday. He was able to spend the first few months of life with them, and I witnessed him being an amazing father. I will forever be grateful to Charlie for giving me my miracle babies. He will always be our forever angel.

Thriving and Surviving

Here I am now, a widow with two infant boys, struggling to believe my new reality. I had to hold onto my faith and trust God despite the immense pain and grief. I first acknowledged my hurt and allowed myself to go through the grieving process. From childhood to adulthood, I have learned the importance of recognizing and confronting my pain as a path to a healthier self. I have thrived through my hardships by choosing perseverance. Life is about choices and how we respond to the events that come our way. Whether dealing with personal loss or life changes that bring anxiety, I have dedicated myself to helping others overcome their struggles. I've continued my life's mission to turn pain into purpose. As the CEO of Lulu Orange, Inc., my passion is to help others achieve their goals. With over two decades of experience in entertainment, healthcare leadership, and pageant coaching, I have learned that we are all working towards success in some form. I see a significant gap in how individuals cope with life's changes.

Not understanding how to cope and respond healthily to obstacles can be detrimental, leading to depression or even suicide. I authored the e-guidebook "*Greatness Lies Within You: A 10- Step Guide to Success That Will Give You the Tools to Achieve Your Goals.*" This guide has been my roadmap, and I travel and speak at events to help others on their journey. If I can do it, so can you.

SECTION FIVE

THRIVING IN
MOTHERHOOD

MOTHERHOOD CHANGED MY LIFE

SANDRINA DAVIS

"Tell the story of the mountain you climbed. Your words could become a page in someone else's survival guide."
– Morgan Harper Nichols

In May 2008, I found myself unexpectedly pregnant—a shock considering the medical advice I had received in my youth. Unmarried and deeply involved in my church, the news brought a complex mix of emotions—shame, guilt, and fear, alongside the quiet promise of new life. That season tested my faith, yet it became a time of necessary spiritual growth, where I felt the unshakable embrace of God's unconditional love.

But on January 1, 2009, at 12:14 AM, I welcomed my son into the world—the first baby born in the hospital that year. As I held him, uncertainty washed over me. How would I manage this new chapter of life? Would I be a good example for him? But one thing was clear: I had to rise, not just for myself but for him. And with that resolve, I embarked on a journey of personal growth and resilience.

Every significant professional achievement I've earned—every degree, every accolade—has come after the birth of my son. That's not a coincidence. His arrival was a turning point, pushing me to lean deeper into God's promise in Romans 8:28: "All things work together for the good of those who love Him." My faith became the bedrock of every decision, and each trial along the way fortified my resolve.

Returning to work after maternity leave was humbling. I found myself in an entry-level role in customer service, but that job became more than just a paycheck—it was where I discovered my love for people and my natural ability to nurture and care for others. I made sure to go beyond my job description, creating a positive and inclusive atmosphere. I didn't just work alongside colleagues; I built a community of support and connection.

At that point, I didn't have a college degree. I had been pursuing a bachelor's degree in business administration, but pregnancy complications forced me to pause. With financial constraints, returning to school wasn't immediately possible, so I pressed on, working to provide for my son.

In September 2011, I re-enrolled in school. But just a week and a half later, my mother—my rock—suffered a stroke in her sleep and passed away. Devastated, I paused my studies again to grieve and take care of family matters. Shortly after, I began working in administration at a non- profit organization—a role that would transform my life.

At the non-profit, I poured my heart into the work, just as I had done before. My colleagues became like family, and I thrived in the environment. Yet, despite my success, I couldn't shake the feeling that there was more for me to accomplish. Every night, I would reflect on how I could do more, be more, and leave a lasting example for my son.

Determined to complete my degree, I re-enrolled again. But life threw another curveball—my father became ill. My studies were once again put on hold, and by the time I was ready to return, I faced a difficult choice: start over or apply for an MBA through prior learning assessment. I chose the latter and was accepted. I dove into my MBA, believing this degree was my key to career advancement. Financial struggles emerged, and I prayed for direction. After much deliberation, I resigned from my job and used my voluntary pension to fund my education. God gave me peace about the decision. In January 2017, I resigned and spent four months unemployed.

During this time, I had one of the biggest revelations of my spiritual journey: promotion comes from God, not man. His approval supersedes all. I was then given the opportunity to serve as General Manager of a non-profit while completing my master's degree. Despite facing rejection from three professional opportunities due to the absence of my degree, I remained undeterred. I knew my worth, even when others didn't see it.

In time, I transitioned into another incredible role as Jamaica Director for a U.S.-based non- profit. With my degree finally in hand, I eventually became the CEO of a local non-profit, making an impact in the lives of thousands. Every victory felt like confirmation that, despite the obstacles, God's plan was still unfolding.

Motherhood was not just a responsibility; it was my motivation and the cornerstone of my resilience. Balancing work, school, and parenting wasn't easy. There were moments of self- doubt—times when my son asked if the children I worked with were more important than him. The balancing act was delicate, but through it all, my faith sustained me.

In the "in-betweens"—those moments of juggling school pickups, late-night work meetings, and bedtime stories—was where I found my true strength. It was in these moments that I learned the most about my capacity to love, lead, and inspire.

Thriving, for me, isn't defined by society's metrics of success. It's about waking up with purpose, knowing I'm exactly where God has called me to be. I see my work not as employment but as a divine mission—a ministry to the broken, the lost, and the overlooked.

To the mother balancing her faith, career, and home life, I offer this advice:

- Put God first always.

- Believe in your own worth even when others don't. You have something unique to offer the world.

- Know your value and give your best effort in every task, no matter how small.

- Embrace your "motherness"—it's a superpower, not a hindrance.

- Pursue your goals relentlessly. Your success is not just for you but for your children too.

- Seek support—from family, friends, or mentors. Surround yourself with positive influences.

- Prioritize self-care—your well-being matters.

- Celebrate the small wins—each step forward is progress.

Motherhood and faith have been my guiding forces, shaping me into the woman, mother, and leader I am today. Thriving is about living out your God-given purpose, and when you do that, no challenge is too great.

MOTHER,
THE UNIVERSAL LANGUAGE

MECHELEY BURTLEY

They say Motherhood is one of the toughest "hoods" in the world. As a mother of 13 years with four children, I wholeheartedly agree with that statement. The endless hours of service, sleepless nights, unexpected emergency room visits, and miracle meals made from a box of rice and canned vegetables—these are experiences many mothers have endured since the beginning of time. The responsibility for another human being's well- being can be overwhelming.

However, we were created for this role, literally. Each year, I become more convinced that I possess strength even when I feel weak. The truth is, the One who creates life has always been with me and my children. Here's a little backstory: I became a mother at 21. I married at 24, and we had two more children during our marriage. Unfortunately, we divorced when I was 28, leaving me as a single mother with three children under the age of seven. A year later, I tried reconciling with my children's father at 29, and we had our fourth child when I was 31. Through this romantic roller coaster, my one constant—besides God—was my role as a mother.

Navigating the journey of motherhood, especially after my divorce, required me to remain rooted and anchored in Christ. No matter where I was emotionally or relationally, I had to be physically and emotionally present for my children. Initially, I wasn't great at this, but I soon learned the importance of balance and made changes to parent from a healthy and whole place. Even as I faced traumatic personal changes, I believe my role as a mother kept me grounded.

I didn't succumb to depression during my divorce because I made a conscious decision not to. There was too much at stake. The responsibility of raising healthy, loving human beings outweighed my disappointment. I had multiple lives depending on me, and that was all I needed to push through any challenge. My role as a mother drove me closer to God because I knew I couldn't give my children the best without Him.

Motherhood has greatly grown my faith. Like most mothers, I wanted to protect my children however I could. But there came a time when I had to put aside my natural strategies and tap into my spiritual defenses. After my divorce, I rented a three-bedroom house on the south side of Chicago. One night, while sleeping on the couch near my children's room, my 3-year-old daughter started whining and rolling in her sleep. I went to check on her, and when I woke her, she looked frightened and told me, "There was a lady in my bed with long black nails trying to pull my panties down. She looked all black, but I couldn't see her face." I noticed her underwear was shifted under her gown. Feeling uneasy, I prayed over her and let her sleep with me that night.

Not long after, while my children's father was watching them, he told me he saw a large black figure—a shadow—walk past him and into our daughter's room. He thought it was me at first, but when he realized it wasn't, he quickly checked her room. No one was there, just our sleeping children. I hadn't yet told him about my daughter's experience, but when I did, he was as concerned as I was. The figure he saw matched the description our daughter had given. I knew it was time to take action spiritually and evict whatever spirit felt it had the right to be in my home. This encounter ignited a desire to pursue a deeper relationship with the Lord.

Growing up in church, I knew about Him, but my knowledge was based on other people's experiences. Now, I wanted to know Him for myself and have Him show up for me and my children in ways I hadn't experienced before. That incident with my daughter was the catalyst for my spiritual awakening and the beginning of my dedication to covering my children spiritually and teaching them to do the same. Once I made that decision, things didn't get easier immediately.

Life still felt heavy, and there was always something on top of my regular responsibilities: working, caregiving, church commitments, and household tasks. I also had to restructure my days to include dedicated time with the Lord, something that should have already been part of my routine. At first, I treated this as just another obligation, which was the wrong mindset. After a few weeks of trying to do everything in my own strength, I still felt like I was drowning.

Then, 1 Peter 5:7 came to mind: "Cast your cares on Him, for He cares for you." The scripture sounded good, but after experiencing deep disappointments from the men in my life, it was hard to believe God truly cared for me. The enemy planted thoughts of doubt in my mind:

Did He care when He let my father die when I was one? Did He care when I was molested? When I got divorced? These thoughts weren't from God but were intended to keep me stuck in disbelief. But as I meditated on scripture and accepted God's love, the enemy's suggestions left me. I learned that "casting" my cares meant giving them to the Lord. The hurt, pain, and trauma weren't mine to bear or fix.

Another scripture that helped me was Proverbs 3:5-6, "Trust in the Lord with all your heart and lean not on your own understanding; in all your ways acknowledge Him, and He will direct your paths." Trusting God not only helped me navigate single motherhood but also allowed me to lead my children in the right direction.

Spiritually, I confessed the Word of the Lord over my children and me, standing in deliverance for us all. Without God, I don't know how I would have made it through that dark, confusing time. Taking on the responsibility for my children's spiritual well-being deepened my faith and made me want to be a better believer. I knew they were watching me, so I wanted to live for Christ and show them by example, not just by words.

Motherhood and Career

Motherhood also had a profound impact on my career. My drive, commitment, and dedication to advancing myself professionally stemmed from being a mother.

Growing up in poverty, I experienced many hardships that I never wanted my children to go through. God desires a life of abundance for us, and I knew I had to work hard to ensure my children had everything they needed, whether or not a man was present. From singing, doing hair, to making cheesecakes, I used every talent I had to create income.

After having children, my desire for financial success increased. When I had my first child at 21, I was a general manager making

$50,000 in 2011, financially independent and doing well for myself. But as the years progressed and the economy changed, I knew I had to get serious about building wealth. In 2018, I started an organization for like-minded women, Mechele's Sister Socials, and began hosting events to build community and generate revenue. After multiple sold-out events, I opened an event space business in 2019. My children were involved in every step, learning the value of service and hard work.

Motherhood made me want to create a legacy. I went to business school, organized my company legally, and laid a foundation not just for my career but also for my children's futures.

Advice for Mothers

Having been a single, married, and divorced mother, I've learned lessons that I hope will help other mothers.

To single mothers: Keep God first. This may sound cliché, but it's the only way to balance being both a woman and a mother. God will align you with the right people, giving you discernment to protect yourself and your children. Avoid temporary fixes like alcohol or shallow relationships. Focus on God, and know that you can do anything with Him by your side.

To married mothers: Your husband should come first after God, even before your children. Your children will create their own families one day and look to your marriage as a blueprint. Teach them the value of family and the importance of healthy relationships by your example.

To working mothers: Go after your dreams! God will give you the desires of your heart. Show your children perseverance and dedication by leading by example.

In conclusion, I pray that something I've said uplifts, strengthens, and encourages you. May generational curses be broken, financial breakthroughs occur, and hearts be healed. The best is yet to come. You are bold, confident, and blessed, and so are your children.

Amen.

OWN YOUR JOURNEY

NICOLE V. LOVETT

My parents introduced me to the world as Nicole Natalie Vanessa Van-Reil, but as I've journeyed through life, I now answer to the name Nicole Van-Reil Lovett. That's who I am known as today. I see myself as a beautiful, courageous, unique, and confident woman of faith. I believe I am a valuable individual, essential to the very fabric of life. I am also a mother of two wonderful young ladies, Charissa Teagan Lovett and Christen Paige Lovett, gifts from God to this generation and the world.

In addition to being a mom, I wear many hats—wife, pastor, entrepreneur, educator in the beauty industry, a newly licensed professional in financial services, and creative director of liturgical dance.

Balancing these roles was already a challenge, but when motherhood was added to the mix, it added yet another layer. I was divided into smaller parts of myself, trying to manage being a wife, leader, business owner, and now, a mother. I can honestly say that I am deeply in love with motherhood—so much so that I can't even imagine my life before my girls existed. However, this new chapter of life has also brought its complexities. It's easy to become overwhelmed if the proper boundaries aren't in place.

Motherhood has certainly impacted my business. It has disrupted my assumptions about time management, leaving me with less time for ministry, business, marriage, personal space, and even my devotion to God. I've had to reevaluate everything, including my income, which has led me to explore new ways of earning that don't rely on trading my time for money. I had to face the reality that I could no longer depend on the active income model I had grown accustomed to. Instead, I had to pursue passive income and rethink what financial stability looked like for the future.

The truth is, being a mom is a full-time job—one that lasts a lifetime. It requires full- time scheduling, commitment, and focus. Without setting healthy boundaries, motherhood can consume your entire life, your thoughts, and your time. So, how do you balance this all-consuming role with everything else you're responsible for?

It is possible to be successful in your career, ministry, and community while striving to meet your motherhood milestones.

However, motherhood often takes precedence over other commitments, and learning to say "no" becomes a necessary skill. Trying to fit your old life into your new reality is like forcing a square peg into a round hole—it just won't work. I had to let go of some commitments and prepare myself to say "no" to opportunities that seemed to be the death of my potential. But through it all, I had to trust in God's perfect timing.

God's timing is always perfect, and I remind myself of that often. Even if I miss an opportunity now, I know that what is meant for me won't pass me by. As Psalm 46:10 reminds us, *"Be still, and know that I am God."* When God opens a door, no one can close it, and when He closes a door, no one can open it. Motherhood may affect every aspect of my life—ministry, business, marriage—but it doesn't define who I am at my core. Over time, I've learned that my identity isn't tied to being an entrepreneur, wife, pastor, or even a mother. These are roles I play, but they are not who I am.

So, who are you? Do you know who you are as an individual, separate from the roles you play? Do the people around you really know you? We often define ourselves by our titles, but our core identity has nothing to do with what we do—it's about knowing our intrinsic worth, our value, and our purpose beyond our responsibilities.

Who were you before the titles and roles? Before the accomplishments and the achievements? If you lose a child, a spouse, or a career, does your identity disappear with them? These are hard questions, but they are essential. Your worth doesn't come from what you do; it comes from who you are at the core of your being.

I am here to remind you: you are not your performance, your job, or your roles. You are a woman, valuable and loved by God, just as you are.

So, strip away the titles. Who are you without them? Practice saying these truths to yourself:

> "I am a woman first."
> "I am special."
> "I am unique."
> "I am beautiful."
> "I am valuable."
> "I am loved."

Who are you as a mother at your core? Remember, you are a confident, courageous woman who just happens to be a mom, a leader, a business owner, a wife, a sister, and a friend. Your identity doesn't come from these roles; it comes from knowing your worth and your purpose in God.

Many of us have experienced trauma that has stripped us of our identity. To heal, we must shift our focus inward and understand that we are not defined by what happened to us. Say it out loud:

> "I am not the pain."
> "I am not the shame."
> "I am not my past."
> "I am not the failure."

Healing begins when we recognize our identity in Christ, not in the things that have happened to us or the roles we play.

I didn't have my first daughter until I was 40, and though some might call me a late bloomer, I wouldn't change a thing. God's timing is perfect. I wasn't mentally, emotionally, or spiritually ready to parent from a healthy place before then. I don't compare myself to my peers whose children are now adults. My journey is mine, and theirs is theirs. Even moments of regret have a purpose in our lives.

When we stop viewing setbacks as failures and start seeing them as moments of purpose, we can move forward without being weighed down by what's behind us. I never wanted to have children just because my biological clock was ticking. Anything built on a flawed foundation will eventually fall. As you move forward in life, I encourage you to find your identity and purpose before stepping into marriage or motherhood. Know who you are, heal from your past, and live from a place of wholeness.

Who you are before these life-changing events is who you will be afterward. Don't expect a new version of yourself to emerge without doing the inner work. Nothing just disappears. It must be addressed.

In life, nothing changes unless we do the work of healing and growth.